Revise

Pearson Edexcel GCSE (9–1)
Citizenship Studies
Revision Guide and Workbook

T0386093

Series Consultant: Harry Smith

Authors: Gareth Davies, Rachel Fletcher, Graeme Roffe

Also available to support your revision:

Revise GCSE Study Skills Guide   9781292318875

The **Revise GCSE Study Skills Guide** is full of tried-and-trusted hints and tips for how to learn more effectively. It gives you techniques to help you achieve your best – throughout your GCSE studies and beyond!

Revise GCSE Revision Planner   9781292318868

The **Revise GCSE Revision Planner** helps you to plan and organise your time, step-by-step, throughout your GCSE revision. Use this book and wall chart to mastermind your revision.

For the full range of Pearson revision titles across KS2, 11+, KS3, GCSE, Functional Skills, AS/A Level and BTEC visit: www.pearsonschools.co.uk/revise

Published by Pearson Education Limited, 80 Strand, London, WC2R ORL.

www.pearsonschoolsandfecolleges.co.uk

Copies of official specifications for all Pearson qualifications may be found on the website: qualifications.pearson.com

Text and illustrations © Pearson Education Ltd 2019

Typeset, illustrated and produced by QBS Learning

Cover illustration by Eoin Coveney

The rights of Gareth Davies, Rachel Fletcher and Graeme Roffe to be identified as authors of this work have been asserted by them in accordance with the Copyright, Designs and Patents Act 1988.

First published 2019

25

16

British Library Cataloguing in Publication Data

A catalogue record for this book is available from the British Library

ISBN 978 1 292 26816 3

Acknowledgements

Text credits: 1: Office for National Statistics (ONS): National Population Projections: 2016-based statistical bulletin www.ons.gov.uk/peoplepopulationandcommunity/populationandmigration/populationprojections/bulletins/nationalpopulationprojections/2016b_sedstatisticalbulletin. Accessed: 1. January 2019. Contains public sector information licensed under the Open Government Licence v3.0. © Crown/Office for National Statistics, 2016; **2: Refugee Council:** Who's who, Definitions © Refugee Council, 2017; **39, 40: Crown Copyright:** Policy paper, Autumn Budget 2017, www.gov.uk/government/publications/autumn-budget-2017-documents/autumnbudget-2017. Accessed: 1. January 2019. Contains public sector information licensed under the Open Government Licence v3.0. © Crown/Office for Budget Responsibility, 2017; **72, 73: Parliamentary Copyright:** Hansard, 31 January 2018 Volume 635 Column 812, para 6, hansard.parliament.uk/commons/2018-01-31/debates/F713776F-A298-.089-8..8-B.01020818B 8/Engagements. Accessed: 1. January 2019. © Parliamentary Copyright, 2018. Contains Parliamentary information licensed under the Open Parliament Licence v3.0.; **93: United Nations:** 'What We Do' tab, www.un.org/en/sections/what-we-do/index.html. Accessed: 1. January 2019. © United Nations 2019.

The author and publisher would like to thank the following individuals and organisations for permission to reproduce photographs:

Photographs

(key: t: top; b: bottom; c: centre; l: left; r: right)

123RF: Donato Fiorentino 85bl; **Alamy Stock Photo:** Mark Sykes 25, PA Images 31c, Richard Bryant/Arcaid Images 34l, Lisa Ryder 34c, Suzanne Plunkett/PA Images 34r, 67photo 57, Jacky Chapman/Janine Wiedel Photolibrary 58l, Mark Harvey 58r, 61, Peter Noyce/Loop Images Ltd 59t, Michael Lusmore 59b, DWD-Comp 60t, Anthony Coleman-VIEW 96; **BPM Media:** 99, 100; **Getty Images:** Rob Stothard/Getty Images Europe 06t, Dan Kitwood/AFP 31b, Daniel Berehulak/Getty Images Europe 62; **Pearson Education Ltd:** Jon Barlow 89, Chris Parker. 2007 92; **Shutterstock:** Ms Jane Campbell 05, David muscroft 06b, 1000 Words 10, Neil Higginson 11, Barry Blackburn 21, Shutterstock 28, Rawpixel.com 52, 120, Fizkes 60b, G. Campbell 64, Maicasaa 82, Andrey_Popov 85bc, Cunaplus 85br, Laurentiu 103, Kstudija 126.

All other images © Pearson Education.

Notes from the publisher

1. While the publishers have made every attempt to ensure that advice on the qualification and its assessment is accurate, the official specification and associated assessment guidance materials are the only authoritative source of information and should always be referred to for definitive guidance.

Pearson examiners have not contributed to any sections in this resource relevant to examination papers for which they have responsibility.

2. Pearson has robust editorial processes, including answer and fact checks, to ensure the accuracy of the content in this publication, and every effort is made to ensure this publication is free of errors. We are, however, only human, and occasionally errors do occur. Pearson is not liable for any misunderstandings that arise as a result of errors in this publication, but it is our priority to ensure that the content is accurate. If you spot an error, please do contact us at resourcescorrections@pearson.com so we can make sure it is corrected.

Websites

Pearson Education Limited is not responsible for the content of any external internet sites. It is essential for tutors to preview each website before using it in class so as to ensure that the URL is still accurate, relevant and appropriate. We suggest that tutors bookmark useful websites and consider enabling students to access them through the school/college intranet.

Contents

. . . .

A small bit of small print

Pearson publishes Sample Assessment Material and the Specification on its website. This is the official content and this book should be used in conjunction with it. The questions in Now try this have been written to help you test your knowledge and skills. Remember: the real assessment may not look like this.

GCSE Citizenship Studies and Brexit

This Revision Guide and Workbook includes revision about the withdrawal of the United Kingdom from the European Union, which was correct at the time of writing.

The changing UK population

Communities develop in the UK as the **composition** (makeup) of the population constantly changes in terms of **age, ethnicity, religion** and **disability**. Government has a responsibility to consider the changing needs of the population, which impacts on plans and voting decisions.

Age

The UK has an **ageing population**, which is predicted to grow in the future. Reasons for this include improved healthcare, better nutrition and a better standard of living. Here are **four** possible impacts of an ageing population:

1. Increased demands on the NHS.

2. Higher cost of social care.

3. Increase in age-related conditions, such as dementia.

4. Raised cost of pensions for longer time periods.

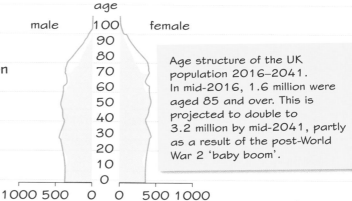

Age structure of the UK population 2016–2041. In mid-2016, 1.6 million were aged 85 and over. This is projected to double to 3.2 million by mid-2041, partly as a result of the post-World War 2 'baby boom'.

population (thousands) in each age band
outline shows year 2041

Ethnicity

Ethnicity in the UK has become **more diverse**. There is growth in dual heritage and multiple identities with parents of different ethnic or religious backgrounds. The government holds a **census** (a survey of the population) every 10 years to find out what changes are taking place. This informs planning and monitoring of equality and discrimination. The 2001 and 2011 census numbers show:

- a decrease in those identifying as White, though this is still over 80%

- an increase in mixed and multiple ethnic groups including Asian/Asian British; Black African/Caribbean/Black British.

Religion

The Universal Declaration of Human Rights states that everyone is free to follow their own religion, or have no faith. The **landscape of religion is changing.** In England and Wales the 2001 and 2011 census numbers show:

- a decrease in those identifying as Christian, though still a majority at over 50%

- an increase in those identifying as Muslim as the second largest religious group

- other main religious groups identifying as Hindu, Sikh, Jewish or Buddhist

- an increase in those declaring that they have no religion, at around 25%

- regional differences, with London as the most diverse, for example.

Disability

Over 11 million people live with disability, impairment or a limiting long-term illness and many require benefits or social care. Those with disability increase with age, rising to over 45% in those over retirement age. Laws such as the UK Equality Act 2010 protect the disabled from discrimination.

Impact of changes on wealth

The **changing composition** of the UK impacts on the distribution of wealth and the rich–poor divide. Increases in benefit sanctions and laws such as the 'bedroom tax', have raised poverty levels. This increases the demand for charities to meet the needs of citizens, such as food banks and homeless shelters.

Now try this

Using an example, explain **one** impact of the way the UK population is changing.   (2)

Migration and its impact

Communities develop as a result of the social, economic and other effects of immigration to the UK.

Reasons why people migrate

Most people migrate for economic, environmental, cultural or political reasons. **Push factors** are reasons to leave a current country. **Pull factors** are reasons to move to a specific country.

Examples of push factors	Examples of pull factors
War or conflict	Economic and work opportunities
Natural disasters	Better standard of living
Religious, ethnic or cultural discrimination	Culture of respect and tolerance
Political persecution or repressive systems	Political stability and increased freedoms
Human rights abuses	Protection of human rights

Migrants coming to the UK

Most people who migrate to the UK fall into **three** categories.

1. **Economic migrants** are people who move to another country for work or economic opportunity, including workers the UK needs.

2. **People seeking asylum (asylum seekers)** leave their country of origin due to a well-founded fear of being persecuted. They have formally applied for asylum in another country but the application is yet to be concluded.

3. **Refugees** are people who have a well-founded fear of being persecuted for reasons of race, religion, nationality or membership of a particular social group or political opinion. They are outside their country of nationality and either unable, or owing to such fear unwilling, to avail themselves of the protection of that country or to return. This also applies to those who may not have a nationality and are outside their country of habitual residence.

UK obligations

The UK has obligations by law to people who are seeking asylum and to refugees. The UK is signatory to the Refugee Convention 1951 to protect refugees. The Human Rights Act 1998 binds the UK by law to recognise human rights such as the right to life, the right to a fair trial and the right to freedom of expression.

Benefits of migration

The social, economic and other effects of migration can be seen as a benefit. For example:

- economic migrants help the economy grow through work, tax, shopping and rent
- migrants may have specialist skills in shortage areas such as doctors or teachers
- diversity, tolerance and respect is enhanced through sharing cultures.

Challenges of migration

Some may see the effects of migration as a challenge, for example:

- population growth makes demands on housing, education, the NHS and may increase unemployment
- rates of pay may reduce if economic migrants work for lower wages
- challenges may cause tensions and increase support for extreme groups.

Now try this

Give **one** reason why the UK is obliged to accept asylum seekers.　(1)

Sources of migration

Sources of migration **from 1945 to the present** include **Commonwealth countries** and **Europe**. Membership of these organisations has increased migration, along with ease of travel and the UK's position in the world. Work and study are key reasons for those now migrating to the UK.

The Commonwealth

The Commonwealth is a key source for migrants to the UK and many prefer the UK because:

- migrants from the same countries are already resident so they join familiar communities.
- they share elements of British culture, British values and the English language.
- they share a history that has created a common identity.
- the UK appealed to Commonwealth countries to help fill job shortages after World War 2.
- the British Nationality Act of 1948 created the status of **Citizen of the United Kingdom and Colonies**, allowing migration to the UK (later revoked by the Immigration Act of 1971).

Commonwealth countries by region (53 member states in 2018)	
Africa	Botswana, Cameroon, The Gambia, Ghana, Kenya, Kingdom of Eswatini, Lesotho, Malawi, Mauritius, Mozambique, Namibia, Nigeria, Rwanda, Seychelles, Sierra Leone, South Africa, Uganda, United Republic of Tanzania, Zambia
Asia	Bangladesh, Brunei Darussalam, India, Malaysia, Pakistan, Singapore, Sri Lanka
Caribbean and the Americas	Antigua and Barbuda, The Bahamas, Barbados, Belize, Canada, Dominica, Grenada, Guyana, Jamaica, Saint Lucia, St Kitts and Nevis, St Vincent and The Grenadines, Trinidad and Tobago
Europe	Cyprus, Malta, United Kingdom
Pacific	Australia, Fiji, Kiribati, Nauru, New Zealand, Papua New Guinea, Samoa, Solomon Islands, Tonga, Tuvalu, Vanuatu

The European Union (EU)

Post-Brexit, members of the EU don't have the same right to live, work and study in the UK, as they did before 2020, but they are still a source of migration because of geographical proximity, a shared European identity, and the English language, widely taught in most schools in Europe.

Member countries of the EU (27 in 2025)			
Austria	Estonia	Italy	Portugal
Belgium	Finland	Latvia	Romania
Bulgaria	France	Lithuania	Slovakia
Croatia	Germany	Luxembourg	Slovenia
Cyprus	Greece	Malta	Spain
Czech Republic	Hungary	Netherlands	Sweden
Denmark	Ireland	Poland	

Some recent history of migration

1945–1949: Polish servicemen for the Allies: thousands resettled in the UK.

1947–1955: Indian immigrants: thousands escaped conflict after the India–Pakistan partition.

1948–1971: Windrush: thousands of Caribbeans filled vacant UK jobs.

1951–1961: Irish immigrants: thousands emigrated from Ireland to the UK.

1972: Ugandan Asian immigrants: thousands of Asians expelled from Uganda given refuge in UK.

1992: EU Treaty of Maastricht: freedom of movement of goods, services, labour, capital.

1998: After Iron Curtain falls: thousands of Eastern Europeans flee persecution for UK asylum.

2004: Eastern European immigrants: EU expansion brought over a million migrants.

Now try this

The following countries are members of the Commonwealth **except** for: **(1)**

☐ **A** Rwanda　　☐ **B** India　　☐ **C** Jamaica　　☐ **D** Latvia

Familiarise yourself with members of the EU and members of the Commonwealth.

Mutual respect

Mutual respect is a central value associated with being a citizen in the UK. It is upheld by legislation and British values to prevent discrimination of minority groups.

Mutual respect in a diverse society

✓ **Mutual respect** is important for understanding the views and beliefs of others, creating the equality and courtesy which are needed for social cohesion.

✓ **Tolerance** is important for the ability to accept and live alongside others who hold beliefs or opinions you may not agree with, to create an inclusive society.

Promoting British values

Individuals who live by basic British values create cohesive communities in the UK. Those who discriminate against others in society don't respect British values. The Department for Education states that all have a duty to promote the British values of:

👍 **democracy**

👍 upholding the **rule of law**

👍 a belief in **individual liberty**

👍 mutual **respect and tolerance** of those with different faiths and beliefs.

Effects of inequality

When an individual, group or community is discriminated against they can become isolated from the community. Examples and effects of inequality and discrimination include:

👎 **the gender pay gap**, meaning men are paid and promoted more than women

👎 **ageism**, e.g. refusal of some medical treatments to those aged 75 and over

👎 **religious discrimination**, e.g. workplaces not accommodating religious customs

👎 **gender reassignment discrimination**, e.g. toilets provided only for men or women.

The role of the Equality Act 2010 in preventing discrimination

The Equality Act 2010 was passed to consolidate previous discrimination acts in the UK, such as the Sex Discrimination Act 1975 and Race Relations Act 1976.

- It prevents discrimination, harassment and unfair treatment of individuals within the nine protected characteristics (shown opposite).

- It protects people in educational establishments, the workplace, public offices, shops or businesses, and on public transport.

Sexual orientation · Age · Disability · Sex · Gender reassignment · Religion or beliefs · Race · Pregnancy and maternity · Marital or civil partnership status

Characteristics protected by the Equality Act 2010

Upholding mutual respect

Here are **three** examples of support for citizens in upholding mutual respect in the UK:

👍 The police monitor and record hate crime, from verbal abuse to physical assault.

👍 Free legal advice for civil law, including discrimination, is provided by Citizens Advice.

👍 Victims of discrimination have an option to pursue complaints through civil courts.

Now try this

Explain **one** way that mutual respect is upheld as a central value underpinning life for UK citizens. (2)

It is important to be able to quote key legislation that refers specifically to discrimination.

Mutual understanding

Mutual understanding underpins a democratic society. It is encouraged in schools and the community through promoting concepts of **diversity**, **integration** and **community cohesion**.

Democratic society

Here are **three** essential concepts that underpin a democratic society:

✓ **diversity**: being part of a community with a range of differences based on culture, religion, class or age

✓ **integration**: bringing communities together and celebrating the diversity of each different group

✓ **community cohesion**: creating communities that are integrated with each other.

The role of schools

Schools play an active role in promoting mutual understanding, through policies of inclusivity. Education and extra-curricular activities promote respect of others, and equality amongst cultures and religions. Schools encourage cohesion through:

- citizenship and RE lessons
- assemblies and religious ceremonies
- learning about religious festivals
- peer education
- projects that challenge discrimination
- cultural events, activities and fundraisers, such as international food days.

Community cohesion

Mutual understanding is encouraged in society so that people live together in harmony, with respect for diversity and for each other.

Features of high levels of cohesion	Features of low levels of cohesion
👍 proactive community action	👎 higher levels of crime
👍 community projects	👎 racism
👍 tolerance of cultural and religious beliefs	👎 gang culture
👍 sense of belonging	👎 segregation of groups
👍 mutual respect	👎 no-go areas
👍 celebration of diversity	👎 increase in extremist views

Community groups

Community projects promote cohesion and are a valuable way for people to interact and improve mutual understanding. They include:

- carnivals and festivals which celebrate diversity
- 'befriend a refugee' projects that help new arrivals
- English language classes to help new arrivals
- projects that bring the generations together.

Events such as the Notting Hill Carnival promote mutual understanding through bringing different ethnicities together and celebrating diversity.

Now try this

Using an example, explain **one** way that schools can promote mutual understanding in society. (2)

Defining identity

A person's identity can be defined in various ways. There are ethnic, religious, gender, age, social, cultural, national, local or regional identities. People will also have multiple identities.

Religious identities

For some citizens of the UK, their **religious identity** is the biggest determining factor of their overall identity. Religious identity can often be shown through dress or symbols, attending places of worship, and following religious traditions.

Religious identity can be seen at the Southwark Eid Festival, held to mark the end of Ramadan, the Muslim month of fasting.

Ethnic and cultural identities

Ethnic and **cultural identities** refer to the groups, history or ethnicity people feel they belong to. This can also be regional or generational.

Traveller communities are an example of ethnic and cultural identity. They have a distinct group identity consisting of a long-celebrated history and lifestyle, and shared values and norms.

Age, gender and social identities

Further forms of identity include:

- **Age**, which changes identity over time. For example, a younger person's identity may be defined by music, sport, lifestyle choices and presence on social media. This contrasts with the shared experience of generations who lived around World War 2. Identity may change through adulthood with jobs, marriage, having a family, and changes during retirement.

- **Gender**, often involving debates around stereotypical male and female roles. For many people their gender, for example transgender or gender neutral, is important to their identity.

- **Social identities**, which are determined by the groups people choose to spend time with, such as sporting communities, peer groups or social media.

National, local and regional identities

Identity may also be defined by:

- **National identity:** all UK citizens with full citizenship status share a national identity, of being British. This is reflected in official documents such as a passport or driving licence

- **Local** or **regional identity:** belonging to England, Scotland, Wales or Northern Ireland, or a smaller geographical region of the UK, might mean more to some people's identity than simply being British. Identifying with what characterises them, and considering their distinctive traditions, culture, language and history can be very important.

Multiple identities

Most people have **multiple identities**. For example, a person with a Scottish mother and Jamaican father may identify with both cultures. A person may be British and Hindu, with an Indian heritage. A person's family identity may be as both a mother and a daughter.

Now try this

Explain **two** ways in which individual identity can change.   (4)

Identity debates

The UK is a **multi-nation state** made up of four nations: England, Wales, Scotland and Northern Ireland, with the UK being the administrative state, and the official nationality being British. This can impact on debates about identity.

Debates about identity

Individuals may identify differently in relation to their UK identity. Some may identify with their nation or with regional identities, rather than their legal identity. For example, they may consider their identity as Welsh rather than British, or as Cornish rather than English. Key factors include shared history, culture and traditions, and language.

Here are some examples.

The four nations comprising the UK

England

- Debates about the English identity include how far it may be seen as interchangeable with the British identity as historically and geographically UK power has been based in the capital, London.

- Media in countries such as the USA often link English identity with cultures and traditions associated with politics and the monarchy, such as the State opening of Parliament, or the changing of the guard.

Wales

- Debates about the Welsh identity include the historic importance of the Welsh language. The Welsh Language Act of 1993 put Welsh on an equal standing with English in all public sectors.

- Cultures and traditions often associated with the Welsh identity include distinctive food (e.g. Welsh cakes), celtic music and Welsh costume.

Scotland

- Debates about the Scottish identity include the desire by many for independence. Scotland has a history of self-rule, resulting in some differences in law and education systems. In 2014 there was a referendum for Scottish independence where 44.7% voted to leave the UK.

- Cultures and traditions often linked with Scottish identity include distinctive food (e.g. haggis), music (e.g. bagpipes) and costume (e.g. kilts).

Northern Ireland (NI)

- Debates about Northern Ireland identity include historic factors such as the partition of Ireland when Northern Ireland remained with the UK in 1921. Religion is also an important part of Northern Ireland identity where they are mainly protestant while Ireland is mainly Catholic.

- Cultures and traditions often linked with Northern Ireland include distinctive food (e.g. colcannon), celtic music and Irish costume.

Now try this

Explain **two** factors that may be important to a person's identity.   (4)

Human and moral rights

Human and **moral** rights in the UK underpin democratic values and duties, and ensure that rights are universal. Every citizen should be treated with tolerance and respect.

Human rights

The **Universal Declaration of Human Rights (UDHR)** was developed by the newly formed United Nations General Assembly in 1948 in response to the horrors of the world wars, especially the genocidal policies of Nazi Germany. It called upon governments to protect and promote individual rights and freedoms, so no citizen would suffer the same fate as the Jews and other victims of the Nazis again. The UDHR has 30 articles, including the rights to:

- life, liberty and security
- freedom from slavery and torture
- equal protection of the law and privacy
- education, freedom of association and of speech, thought, opinion, conscience and religion.

Human Rights Act 1998

The Human Rights Act 1998 enshrined the UDHR into British law and complied with the European Convention on Human Rights. However, some argue that human rights are not upheld in all areas of society, for example:

- sentenced prisoners are not allowed to vote and participate in free elections in the UK, although the European Convention on Human Rights states that everyone can vote, even those in prison.
- homeless people living on the streets are denied Article 25, the right to a basic standard of living, which includes housing.

Moral rights and duties

Moral rights are not laws or punishable by the courts, but **generally acceptable standards** that the majority adhere to. For example, the behaviours below are reasonably expected, so there is a moral right, even though there is no legal right or duty. For example, helping others in need, someone at risk of injury, or someone who is worse off than you. Other behaviours to **avoid** could include:

- lying
- cheating or plagiarism (e.g. in exams, or a creative artist taking credit for other people's work)
- wasting time at work doing non-work activities
- using your position of power for your own advantage.

Upholding rights

Rights of different people or groups (nationally and locally) can come into conflict and need to be balanced in different situations in life and work where there is inequality or unfairness. Here are three examples.

1. **Suspected terrorists.** In 2008, Gordon Brown proposed a 42-day detention without charge for suspected terrorists. This was defeated in the House of Lords.

2. **Extremist groups.** National Action is a far-Right group formed in 2013. Due to its racist propaganda and activities, it was proscribed as a terrorist group in 2016, which makes it a criminal act to belong to, promote meetings or wear clothing or display articles which show support.

3. **The Investigatory Powers Act 2016.** Known also as the 'snooper's charter', this ensures that government agencies and security services can access the phone and computer browsing history of citizens with a judge's permission.

Now try this

Explain **two** rights that some feel are denied in the UK.　(4)

Legal rights

Legal rights in the UK are created, enforced and protected by government. They also require the responsibility of individuals to obey the law and respect the freedoms of others.

- Many human rights become legal rights when a law is put in place to protect them.
- Legal rights enable society to function in a regulated way with appropriate safeguards.
- Many legal rights affect daily life, as some have age restrictions relating to responsibility.

Some key age laws	Age allowed
Age of criminal responsibility	10 (8 in Scotland)
To get a part-time job	13
Age of consent and marriage with parental permission; to give personal consent to medical, dental, surgical treatment; choose a GP; get a national insurance number, cash ISA, premium bonds; buy a pet; buy lottery tickets; drive a moped; apply for a passport; apply for legal aid	16
To drive a car; become a blood donor	17
To vote/stand in elections; serve on a jury; make a will; get married; open a bank account; buy fireworks, tobacco and alcohol	18

Employment law

Legal rights protect citizens in the workplace to ensure people are treated fairly at work, and to avoid conflict. Many laws regarding the workplace were fought for by the Labour Party and the trade union movement, and further developed through EU legislation. They have been created to provide protection in a wide range of employment situations such as unfair dismissal, wage disputes and redundancy. Citizens Advice and trade unions provide advice on employment and discrimination laws.

Consumer law

Consumer law protects the rights of consumers when purchasing goods or services in the UK. **The Consumer Rights Act 2015** declares that:

- goods or services purchased should be as advertised and fit for purpose
- services should be undertaken with reasonable care and skill
- customers can expect to have an exchange or their money back if goods are not as advertised, or repeated if service is unreasonable.

Employment legislation

Key employment legislation includes:

- **Minimum wage laws** to protect employees from exploitation.
- **Health and safety laws** to protect employees and employers in the workplace.
- **Contracts of employment** to define the expectations of employee and employers.
- **The Equality Act 2010** to protect everybody from discrimination in the workplace.

Consumer organisations

Organisations that help citizens with consumer law issues include:

- **Citizens Advice:** offering free advice for **all** aspects of civil law.
- **Trading Standards:** an organisation that investigates consumer law complaints.
- **Advertising Standards Authority (ASA):** responds to complaints to ensure advertisements are not misleading, harmful, offensive or irresponsible.

Now try this

Using an example, explain how consumer law protects the rights of consumers. (2)

Political rights

The political rights of citizens in the UK underpin its democratic values. Participating in political life requires responsible action from citizens.

Democratic values

The UK is founded on fundamental rights, laws and principles which all citizens should respect and adhere to. In a political state the size of the UK this is managed by a system of **representative democracy**, which means:

- a range of political and social views are represented through different political parties
- minority parties such as the Monster Raving Loony Party and the British National Party may stand equally alongside traditional political parties such as Conservative and Labour
- free, confidential and fair elections take place
- citizens elect representatives whose views they agree with, to make decisions on their behalf.

UK citizens visit a polling station to cast votes. Some argue the voting age should be lowered from 18 to 16. At this age citizens are considered responsible enough to give personal consent for medical treatment and to choose their GP. Some argue that the party elected would be in power when 16-year-olds reach the age of 18, so their policies will have a significant impact on their lives.

Political rights for adults

Here are **six** key political rights of adult citizens in the UK:

1. to vote in general elections for a Member of Parliament (MP) to represent them in the House of Commons at Westminster
2. to vote in local elections for councillors to represent them on the local council
3. to vote in referendums, with a single vote on a single issue
4. in some nations, to vote for devolved assemblies and parliaments
5. in some regions, to vote for the Mayor, and/or Police and Crime Commissioner
6. to stand for election as a local councillor, MP, Mayor, or Police and Crime Commissioner.

Political rights for all citizens

All citizens have the right to protest and to:

- **lobby** a Member of Parliament
- **form a pressure group** to change public policy
- **organise a campaign** including leaflets, posters or social media
- **organise a public meeting** or protest
- **petition** traditionally or online. If signatures exceed 100,000, the issue is considered for debate in Parliament.

Citizen's responsibilities

Citizens have certain responsibilities:

- to vote as a civic duty
- to use voting as an opportunity to be educated and informed about issues
- to use voting to ensure governments keep their promises and are accountable
- to vote so outcomes represent the population
- if protesting, to do so legally
- to use freedom of speech but not offend.

Now try this

Identify **two** different elections that an adult in the UK can vote in.   (2)

The rule of law

The rule of law is essential to uphold the rights and duties of citizens in a democratic society. It is also important to have a system of checks and balances to ensure that human rights debates regarding privacy, freedom of speech, and the threat of terrorism are considered.

The rule of law

The rule of law has **three** basic principles:

1. **Equality before the law.** This ensures that everybody is treated equally in the legal system and that no-one is above the law. For example, some serving Members of Parliament were imprisoned over an expenses scandal that emerged in 2009.

2. **Innocent until proven guilty.** In criminal law, everyone is considered innocent until proven guilty beyond reasonable doubt in a court of law.

3. **Access to justice.** Everybody has the right to use the justice system. In reality, cuts to legal aid have limited access to justice for the poorest in society, especially in civil court cases for family law or cases that involve those under the age of 18.

The **rule of law** applies equally to all citizens, whatever their status. Everyone must obey the law and has the right to be protected by it. It ensures fairness and respect for human rights within the legal system.

Human rights checks and balances

The Human Rights Act 1998 specifies the rights UK citizens have within the law. There are debates about how rights and freedoms need to be **limited** for the good of the majority. Here are **three** examples.

1. **The right to privacy**
   Many tabloids intrude on the lives of celebrities to gain a story. This freedom has been limited so it does not breach the right to privacy. For example, in 2011 *The News of the World* was closed over a scandal where journalists hacked the voicemail of celebrities and missing student, Milly Dowler.

2. **Freedom of speech**
   Freedom of speech may be misused to promote extremist views. This should be limited so it protects rights and does not discriminate against others. For example, in 2016, a British neo-Nazi group, National Action, was identified as a terrorist group and banned under the Terrorism Act 2000.

3. **Terrorism threats**
   Suspected terrorists can be held and questioned without charge for an extended period of 14 days. This limits the right of individuals to liberty for the perceived protection of the public. There have been many failed political attempts to increase the length of time to 90 days.

Now try this

Identify **one** of the principles of the rule of law in the UK.   (1)

Magna Carta and developing rights

The Magna Carta is seen as the first step towards the democratic state we live in today and the origins of justice in our legal system.

Justice replacing arbitrary rule

The Magna Carta (Latin for 'Great Charter') was signed by King John in 1215, and is a charter of liberties granted to the English people. It contained 63 agreements which essentially ended the absolute power of the monarch. This came about because of **three** key things:

1. King John was seen as a tyrannical leader. He funded the unsuccessful Battle of Bouvines through taxation that the barons, who were wealthy men, felt was unfair. The barons' land had been granted by the King in return for their loyalty and support.

2. In 1213 King John interfered with the church, rejecting the appointment of Stephen Langton as Archbishop of Canterbury. King John was excommunicated by the Pope, who also banned people in England from receiving sacraments and being buried in consecrated ground.

3. King John failed to meet the barons so they switched allegiance to Robert Fitzwalter as leader instead. When they captured the City of London, King John was left with no alternative than to meet and resolve his issues with the barons and archbishops. They met at Runnymede in June 1215, bringing about the agreements in the Magna Carta.

Significance of the Magna Carta and rights today

The key principles of the Magna Carta informed the development of rights today. They are at the core of the United States Bill of Rights approved in 1791, the Universal Declaration of Human Rights 1948 and the European Convention on Human Rights 1953.

Key principles in the Magna Carta	Key principles in rights today
• The Church could appoint its own bishops and archbishops free from interference from the King.	• To acknowledge the rights of individuals and to limit the authoritarian powers of the monarchy.
• The King could not demand taxes without agreement from barons and bishops, and all regions had to pay the same tax.	• To have fairness and limits to taxation.
• The King could not put barons on trial in secret – they must be tried by their peers – and free men (barons, knights, bishops, priests and merchants) could not be arrested or imprisoned without a fair trial.	• That all individuals should have access to justice and a fair trial by their peers.
• Everybody was subject to the law, including the King.	• To follow the rule of law that everyone is subject to the law and no-one is above the law.

Now try this

Identify **two** links the Magna Carta has with the UK's current legal system.   (2)

Protecting rights and freedoms

Human rights have developed since World War 2. Citizen's rights and freedoms worldwide are protected by the Universal Declaration of Human Rights 1948. Political organisations and individual countries have protected human rights further through conventions and legislation.

Development of key human rights legislation

You need to know the rights and freedoms protected by the following.

UDHR – Universal Declaration of Human Rights 1948

- Created in the wake of the horror of the holocaust during World War 2.
- The United Nations drew up 30 articles to establish rights that every human is entitled to (see page 14).

ECHR – European Convention on Human Rights 1953

- Provides protections for UK citizens.
- Ratified by the newly created Council of Europe, the expectation was that all member states would adhere to and ratify this human rights convention.
- It also established the **European Court of Human Rights**.

UNCRC – United Nations Convention of the Rights of the Child 1990

- Recognises that children under the age of 18 are more vulnerable.
- Sets out the rights that every such child should be entitled to, such as law and order, family life, education and so on.

HRA – Human Rights Act 1998

- UK Act which ratified the European Convention on Human Rights (ECHR) into UK law.
- Allows UK citizens to raise human rights issues and seek resolution in UK courts to uphold these rights.

The future of UK rights

As Prime Ministers, David Cameron and then Theresa May criticised the UK Human Rights Act. Their view was that it offers too many protections to terrorists and foreign serious criminals. Both proposed the idea of a 'British Bill of Rights' which would be up to date and tailored to British society.

Now try this

Which Act ratified the European Convention on Human Rights into UK Law?   (1)

A Universal Declaration of Human Rights 1948

B United Nations Convention of the Rights of the Child 1990

C Human Rights Act 1998

D Equality Act 2010

Protecting human rights

The Universal Declaration of Human Rights 1948 protects freedoms worldwide with 30 articles that every human is entitled to.

1 Freedom and equality	2 Human rights, free from discrimination	3 Life, liberty and security	4 Freedom from slavery	5 Freedom from torture
6 A legal identity	7 Equality before the law	8 A tribunal for violated rights	9 Freedom from arbitrary arrest, detention or exile	10 A fair trial
11 Innocent until proven guilty	12 Privacy	13 Freedom of movement in and out of country	14 To seek asylum	15 A nationality
16 Marriage and family life	17 To own property	18 Freedom of thought, conscience and religion	19 Freedom of expression	20 Freedom of peaceful assembly and association
21 Participation in politics	22 Social security	23 To work	24 Leisure and free time	25 Standard of living including housing and healthcare
26 Free education	27 Cultural life	28 Rights protected by law	29 Protect the rights of others	30 No one can deny you your rights

Summary of the 30 articles of the UDHR 1948. Rights can have a fundamental link to responsibilities. For example, rights protected by the law link to the responsibility to obey the law; rights to participate in politics link to responsibilities to vote.

Now try this

Identify **two** human rights that support democracy.   (2)

Citizens and local government

Local democracy works through a political structure in which local government (local councils and county councils) represent their community and provide local services for citizens.

1 **Central government, based in Westminster** passes national laws, including international relations, defence, national security, immigration, nuclear energy, broadcasting, taxation, social security and has devolved responsibilities for England.

2 **Devolved assemblies and parliaments** such as those of Wales, Scotland and Northern Ireland are responsible for national legislation not covered by Westminster (see page 50).

3 **Regional bodies** have responsibilities such as the election of police and crime commissioners. Some cities have an elected Mayor. For example, an elected Mayor is responsible for economic, social and environmental improvements in the Greater London Authority.

4 **County councils** are responsible for areas such as education, the fire service, libraries, social care, transport and highways.

5 **Local councils such as district, unitary and borough councils** have responsibilities that include collection of council tax and rates, social housing, leisure services, local planning and refuse collection.

6 **Parish and town councils** are responsible for specific local services such as allotments, parks and community centres.

Local council and county council structures

Local councils and county councils are organised in the same way as central government.

In **county councils**, electoral areas are called **divisions**. Most local councillors represent a political party. The party that wins the most seats forms a cabinet to take responsibility for each area of the council's work.

In **local councils**, the electoral areas are called **wards**. The Local Government Act 2000 states that local authorities must follow one of the following structures: a mayor and cabinet executive; a leader and cabinet executive; a committee system.

Roles and responsibilities of local and county councils

There are **three** key roles within a local and county council.

1 **Mayors:** These are either **elected mayors**, such as the Mayor of Greater London, who are elected by the public and responsible for local services, for example; **traditional civic mayors,** who are elected by councillors. They carry out ceremonial duties and chair meetings, but cannot make individual decisions about council business.

2 **Local councillors:** These are elected by the public, and are responsible for representing their party and ward; responding to the needs of residents, in areas such as social housing, leisure services, developing and reviewing council policies, scrutinising the work of the council or cabinet, and community engagement and leadership.

3 **Local officers:** These are employed to work for the council, in partnership with local councillors. They are often responsible for detailed decisions on how council plans are implemented (e.g. the most efficient route for a recycling vehicle).

Now try this

Explain **two** services that can be provided by a district council.   (4)

Paying for local services

Local councils and county councils need funds to pay for the services they provide. This is obtained through council tax, business rates, government grants and income from charges. Factors that affect decision-making when managing the budget to meet needs might include:

- priority spending on key areas such as education and social care
- trading off other areas of spending (e.g. leisure) to create funds for priority spending
- targeting spending for needs specific to local areas (e.g. inner city, suburb, small town, rural).

Council tax

Here are **five** key facts about council tax.

1. Council tax is collected by district, borough and unitary authorities.

2. The amount a council can collect as council tax is set by central government and can be capped.

3. A proportion of this money is collected for county council services such as the police and fire service, and for town or parish council services such as maintenance of parks.

4. Every household must pay council tax, with costs based on home value.

5. The revenue collected by councils can vary, as more affluent areas pay more than deprived areas.

Business rates

Here are **five** key facts about business rates.

1. The amount of business rates paid is determined by the open market rental value of the buildings they operate from.

2. Central government sets business rates.

3. Under the **Local Government Finance Act 2012**, local councils were given the power to keep half of the business rates collected in order to encourage new businesses, perhaps by regenerating a shopping area to attract new retailers.

4. The other half of the money is given to central government and distributed nationally as grants to councils depending on need.

5. If businesses such as shops close down and no longer pay rates, the amount reduces.

Central government grants

Here are **five** key facts about central government grants funding of councils.

1. Central government provides grants to local government (local councils and county councils) each financial year.

2. Some of the funds allocated are for services which must be provided, such as education and social care.

3. The money given to each local authority is calculated on area needs.

4. Austerity plans in recent years saw a 37% reduction of local government grants between 2010 and 2015.

5. Local councils therefore have to plan carefully where their funding will be spent.

Income from charges and fees

Here are **five** key facts about council charges and fees.

1. Councils can make charges and fees for some council services.

2. These could include parking fees on council land and for bulky refuse collection.

3. Charges could include admission to local leisure centres, for example.

4. Some councils charge rent for a stock of council or social housing, though they also have responsibility to maintain them to a 'decent home' standard.

5. There are services that councils are **not** allowed to charge for, which includes education, elections, standard refuse collection, and libraries.

Now try this

Explain **one** way that encouraging the development of local business and enterprise would benefit local government funds or income.

(2)

Short answer questions

In the exam, **Paper 1** is **1 hour 45 minutes** and worth **80 marks** in total. In **Section A**, questions are focused on **Theme A: Living together in the UK**.

> ## Paper 1 Section A short answer questions
>
> Short answer questions require you to demonstrate your knowledge and understanding of citizenship concepts, terms and issues. Here are command words you might see:
>
> - **which, give, identify, name**: you need to give a point or example without further development.
> - **explain**: you need to make a point and then develop it to show your understanding.
> - **suggest**: you need to show your understanding where reasons are less clear cut.

Worked example

Which of the following can only be done legally once you are at least 18? **(1)**

☐ A Invest in a cash ISA
☒ B Vote in local government elections
☐ C Get a National Insurance number
☐ D Choose your own GP

Select the right answer. Here, B is correct. The minimum age for the other activities is aged 16.

Give **two** reasons why the UK population has increased by approximately 8 million since 2001. **(2)**

1 The population has increased because of higher levels of immigration than emigration.

2 Medical improvements have resulted in increased longevity for many older people.

'Give' questions test your knowledge and recall.

When questions ask for **two** areas, issues, reasons or ways, give two that are **clearly different**.

Only give the number of reasons requested and not more. Use your time wisely.

Using an example, explain what is meant by 'economic migrant'. **(2)**

An economic migrant is a person who has moved to another country for work. For example, moving to the UK to meet needs for workers such as medical staff or seasonal farm workers.

'Explain' questions require you to demonstrate your understanding.

You must explain the term **and** give an appropriate example. Be careful not to confuse the terms 'economic migrant', 'asylum seeker' and 'refugee' (see page 2).

Suggest **two** reasons for reducing the voting age from 18 to 16. **(2)**

1 Sixteen-year-olds can pay taxes and should have a say in how money will be spent.

2 They are old enough to get married and so should be mature enough to vote.

'Suggest' questions test your understanding and require you to surmise why something may be the case as it is less clear cut.

Make sure you suggest **two** clearly different reasons.

Now try this

Name one piece of legislation that prevents discrimination in the UK.

Source A questions 1

In **Paper 1, Section A**, you will need to apply knowledge and understanding of citizenship concepts, terms and issues to contexts and actions as you respond to a source.

Paper 1 Section A Source A questions

One question in **Section A: Living together in the UK** is based on Source A. You will need to read the source and then answer a question about it. Here are command words you might see:

- **explain:** you need to provide a reasoned explanation that shows your understanding through justifying or giving examples of the points you have identified, applied to a source.

- **compare:** you need to compare two or more issues, opinions or situations.

Source A

Study Source A and then answer the question on the next page.

Source A: The population of New Zealand, 1960-2018

Year	Population*	Urban %
2018	4,750,000	86
2000	3,850,000	85.7
1980	3,150,000	83.4
1960	2,400,000	76.0

*Figures are rounded up or down

New Zealand has a land area of 263,310 km², <u>almost 15,000 km² more than the UK, but the population is only a twelfth of the UK's</u>. Like the UK, it has two main islands and many smaller ones. The largest, North Island, is home to over 75% of the population.

By 2050, the population is expected to reach 5,800,000, of whom more than 90% will live in urban areas. <u>The median age in 2018 was 37.8 but it is expected to exceed 43 by 2050</u>. There is a slight imbalance between the sexes, with 49% of the population being male. <u>Estimated life expectancy at birth in 2018 was 80.5 for males and 84 for females.</u>

<u>Migration contributes significantly to population growth</u>. In 2017, the net increase was 70,000 with 130,000 immigrants but only 60,000 emigrants. <u>There is a strict immigration quota system. Priority is given to migrants possessing skills needed</u> in New Zealand. Applicants exceed the quota so qualified applicants have to ballot for places. Currently, the <u>greatest proportion of migrants come from Asian and Pacific nations</u>.

In 2018, 20% of the population was aged under 15 and 15% were over 65. The birth rate is declining and, <u>like most developed countries, there is a fairly low death rate</u>. The ethnic origin of the population is 75% European, 15% Maori (indigenous New Zealanders), 12% Asian and 7% Pacific. The remainder come from other areas or have not disclosed their ethnicity.

Read the source carefully. It relates to the question on page 19 which is about comparing the population in New Zealand with the population in the UK.

Underlining key points can help focus your answer. Here, for example, consider similarities and differences relating to:
- island structure, size and population
- age
- migration policies
- diversity.

You don't need to know more about New Zealand than is in the source. It prompts you to make some connections with what you have learned about the UK.

Now try this

After reading the source, suggest **one** similarity and **one** difference between the UK and New Zealand populations.

Source A questions 2

This response to a **compare** question relates to Source A on page 18. It shows the qualities your answer to a 'compare' question should demonstrate:

- detailed knowledge about the concepts, terms and issues relevant to the question
- good understanding of how they apply by effective and sustained comparisons between the two contexts.

Worked example

Source A gives you some information about New Zealand and its population. Compare the situation in New Zealand with what you know about the population in the UK.

(6)

 This question relates to Source A on page 18.

The population of New Zealand is much smaller than the UK, even though its area is slightly larger. The UK population has grown rapidly, by about 8 million since 2000, while New Zealand grew by about 1 million. The numbers are smaller but the increase is much faster.

 You should show that you are using the source **and** applying your own knowledge about the UK.

In the UK, the main reasons for population growth are increased life-expectancy and immigration. There was a bulge in the birth rate after World War 2, and many born then are still alive. Thanks to medical advances and better nutrition they are living longer. Life expectancy in New Zealand today is roughly the same as in the UK. New Zealand has a slightly younger population than the UK. The median age in New Zealand is around 38, meaning that half the population is older than 38, but the UK median is 40.

 This offers a coherent explanation of what has occurred.

Both countries experience a net migration benefit, meaning that more people enter the country each year than leave it. In the UK, most migration comes from the EU or the Commonwealth. In New Zealand, the main migration comes from Asian and Pacific countries. Immigration is a concern to both countries. New Zealand has a strict quota system. The number of immigrants is limited each year and preference is given to people with skills which will benefit the economy. The UK has given unrestricted entry to EU citizens, but a points system for non-EU migrants, to encourage people with desirable skills.

 This is a good interpretation of the source, with an explanation.

 A conclusion is not given, as a 'compare' question does not require a conclusion.

Now try this

Explain two problems that come with an ageing population such as that of the UK and New Zealand.

 You could examine problems for the state, for the older people themselves, or for their families. The question is about ageing populations generally, something experienced by both countries.

19

Practice short answer questions

Practise for **Paper 1, Section A,** with these exam-style short answer questions. Example answers are provided (page 132 forward).

Guided

Which of these is a human right protected by UK law?   **(1)**
The right to:

☐ **A** choose the school you attend
☐ **B** use any amount of force to protect property
☐ **C** be treated fairly and without discrimination
☐ **D** drive a car when you are 17.

Read the question and possible answers carefully before selecting your answer.

Give **one** benefit to the UK of migration.   **(1)**

....

....

....

Only provide one benefit. You do not need to develop the point.

Suggest **two** reasons why the income of many local councils has been reduced in real terms in the last 10 years.   **(2)**

1 ....

....

....

2 ....

....

....

'Suggest' questions test your understanding as well as your knowledge.

Using an example, explain **one** way in which the role of a directly elected mayor is different from that of a traditional mayor.   **(2)**

....

....

....

Only explain **one** point, **and** support it with an example.

Explain **two** reasons why it is necessary to show respect for fellow citizens   **(4)**

1 ....

....

....

2 ....

....

....

Show you understand the meaning of respect. Explain **two** clearly **different** reasons. For each one, make a point and then develop it.

Practice Source A questions

Practise for **Paper 1, Section A**, with this exam-style source question. Apply your knowledge and understanding of citizenship concepts, terms and issues in the context of the source. No conclusion is required. Example answers are provided (page 132 forward).

Guided

Study Source A and then answer the question below.

Source A: The financial crisis in local government

It is estimated that damage caused by potholes costs English drivers a total of £1.7m annually.

Local authorities in England are on their knees because of a funding crisis. Surrey's Tory Council faces about £100 million deficit. Northants Council, also under Tory control, issued a section 114 notice stopping new spending because their financial reserves are exhausted. It may be forced to sell its new £53 million headquarters, which only opened in 2017. Newcastle-upon-Tyne's council estimates a 'loss' of about £300 million by 2020.

Some blame this crisis on the austerity measures of the 2010 Coalition Government. Central government funding for local government was cut by 27%. Others say it was caused by waste and poor management, pointing to the fact that some councils pay their Chief Executives more than the Prime Minister. A Minister said that since local authorities set their own spending priorities, they have the power to ease matters by cutting unnecessary spending.

Councils blame government ministers for increasing their statutory duties while cutting their financial contributions. Councils' average spending power has been halved since 2010. They say their financial problems have been ignored and the government has failed to produce a workable solution.

At first, councils cut optional services like leisure, libraries and cultural grants. Now it is essential services like roads and care for the elderly. The system will grind to a halt unless drastic action is taken.

Source A indicates that local government is facing a financial crisis.

Using Source A, explain why this financial crisis has occurred.

(6)

- Read the source and question carefully. Underline relevant information in the source to help you focus your answer.
- Add your own knowledge to what you learn from the source.

Look at what any photographs and captions tell you. Here, the poor road conditions show you something about the state of local government finances. The caption gives information about who ultimately pays for the lack of funding.

Consider why the author names 'Tory' councils, and the relevance of the cost of the headquarters.

Consider:
- how the Tories dominated the Coalition Government.
- the relevance of referring to the salaries of Chief Executives.
- the accuracy of what the minister said about local authority spending.

Consider where councils get their funding from, and whether it is only from the government.

Comment on the difference between 'optional' and 'essential' services.

Use a separate piece of paper to answer this question.

Major political parties

Political parties are groups of people who share political views and goals.

The UK's major political parties hold key philosophical differences about how society would improve under their leadership which they present when standing for a general election.

- A political party's aim is to win a majority in a general election and form a government.
- Most parties are ideological and members share political beliefs. For example, the Scottish National Party, Plaid Cymru, and the Democratic Unionist Party represent national interests, and the Green Party and UKIP focus on issues.
- At elections each party presents a **manifesto** stating policies they would implement.

Major political parties sit on the **political spectrum** that runs from left-wing to right-wing.

LEFT WING ⟶				RIGHT WING
Communism	Socialism	Liberalism	Conservatism	Fascism
A system in which all resources in a nation are owned by the state and shared amongst all the people.	A system of common ownership, offering more equality in society, and robust welfare for those in need.	Belief in individual rights and less government interference. Laws should only be passed to improve society.	Belief in tradition, family values and authority. Advocates of private ownership and free enterprise.	An authoritarian and nationalistic system, typically run by a dictator using force.
	Labour	Liberal Democrats	Conservatives	

Here are some examples of key policies of the main parties.

Issue	Labour Party	Liberal Democrats	Conservative Party
Key principles	Formed to represent the working classes. Responsible for implementing the welfare state and NHS.	Formed to represent middle ground between Labour and Conservatives.	Formed with main principles to protect British culture and traditions, promoting private ownership and private enterprise.
Education	Create a National Education Service that provides free education.	Reinstate university grants for the poorest students.	Create more selective schools to improve standards.
Health	Increase tax bill of top earners to fund NHS.	Tax everyone more to fund NHS.	Real terms increase in NHS spending.
Economic	Reinstate public ownership of sectors like the railways. Increase taxation of the richest.	Boost the economy with a programme of capital investment.	Increase free trade, limit welfare, and decrease government spending.
Social	Extend welfare to meet need; promote equality.	Reverse the cuts to benefits for ages 18–21.	Encourage more home ownership.

Now try this

Identify a feature of the education policy of each of **two** of the major political parties. (2)

How candidates are selected

There are 650 Members of Parliament (MPs). Each one represents a particular part of the country (their **constituency**). A person wishing to become an MP puts themselves forward as a **candidate** who can be **selected** and voted for in a competitive process (an **election**).

Eligible to be a candidate

An individual **can** put themselves forward to stand as a candidate if they are:

- ✓ aged 18 or over
- ✓ a British citizen
- ✓ an Irish citizen
- ✓ an eligible Commonwealth citizen
- ✓ nominated by 10 electors in the constituency they wish to represent
- ✓ able to pay a £500 deposit (returned if over 5% of votes are won)
- ✓ authorised to stand for a political party OR choosing to be an independent candidate.

Not eligible to be a candidate

An individual **cannot** stand as a candidate if they are:

- a civil servant
- a member of the police force
- a member of the armed forces
- a government-nominated director of a commercial company
- a judge
- a peer in the House of Lords
- a Church of England bishop
- the subject of bankruptcy restrictions
- someone who has been convicted and imprisoned for over a year
- someone who has been found guilty of electoral corruption within the last five years.

How candidates are selected

The process below shows how people can become a general election candidate for any of the major parties. Many start their political career at university.

| Many people join and become politically active in their chosen party. |

⬇

| Parties advertise for candidates, and those who are interested and **eligible** apply. |

⬇

| Parties may have a list of prospective candidates who are politically active or advisors on areas of policy. |

⬇

| Prospective candidates try to gain (**canvass** for) votes through interviews, public speaking at meetings (**hustings**), and working for the party in their local constituency. |

⬇

| Local party workers draw up a shortlist. |

⬇

| Local party members vote for the candidate to represent that constituency and the one with the most votes is **selected**. If a constituency typically votes for a political party, it may be viewed as secure by that party and known as a **safe seat**. |

Now try this

Give **two** criteria a person would have to meet to stand as a candidate in a British general election. **(2)**

The concept of democracy

Democracy stems from the politics of ancient Greece and means 'rule of the people, by the people'. In the UK, it describes a system of government where citizens elect political representatives. This includes **representative democracy** (via elections) and **direct democracy** (via referendums). Each has strengths and weaknesses.

Representative democracy

Most western nations operate a system of **representative democracy**. The UK is divided into **650 constituencies** (voting areas), and each constituency elects a Member of Parliament to represent them in the House of Commons. Most elected MPs represent the main political parties.

Strengths of representative democracy	Weaknesses of representative democracy
👍 Every citizen can have a say in who represents them.	👎 Elections mostly take place every five years, which limits citizen input.
👍 If there is a high turnout, parliament is more representative of the public's opinions.	👎 Most MPs will vote with their party rather than represent their constituency.
👍 Constituents can lobby their local MP through locally held surgeries.	👎 The constituents whose party didn't win often feel unrepresented by government.
👍 A local MP will be very aware of the needs of their constituents.	👎 Many MPs may be university educated, so not always representative of constituents.

Direct democracy

The UK uses a system of **direct democracy** for specific issues that need public input. In the UK, the form of direct democracy is called a **referendum**, where citizens vote on a **specific issue**. Referendums are rare in the UK, but some recent ones include:

- **2016**: UK to leave/remain in European Union (EU): outcome – leave 51.9%, remain 48.1% (turnout 72%)
- **2014**: Scottish Independence: outcome – no 55%, yes 45% (turnout 84%)
- **2011**: Change voting system from first past the post (FPTP) to alternative vote (AV): outcome – no 68%, yes 32% (turnout 41%)
- **1975**: UK to remain in European Economic Community (EEC): outcome – yes 67%, no 33% (turnout 65%)

Strengths of direct democracy	Weaknesses of direct democracy
👍 Referendums give government a clear directive from the citizens on an issue.	👎 Often issues are more complex than just a simple yes/no vote.
👍 Every voter can have a say on a particular, usually controversial, issue.	👎 Not every citizen who votes understands the complexity of issues.
👍 Gives government a mandate for action.	👎 The media can influence the electorate.
👍 The most democratic way to make a decision.	👎 If results are close, many may be unhappy.

Now try this

Explain **two** disadvantages of representative democracy in the UK.   **(4)**

General elections

A general election gives people an opportunity to vote for their Member of Parliament (MP) in the 650 **constituencies** (voting areas) in the UK. Elected MPs represent their constituency in the House of Commons at Westminster.

Frequency of general elections

There are **three** key facts about the frequency of general elections in the UK:

1. Under the Fixed Term Parliaments Act 2011, a general election takes place at least every five years on the first Thursday in May.

2. If there is a 'vote of no confidence' in the current government, an earlier election can be called.

3. The House of Commons can vote to hold an election at any time with a two-thirds majority.

The UK operates a **first-past-the-post (FPTP) voting** system. This means that the candidate with the most votes overall in a constituency is elected as MP. To form a **majority** government, a party must win in 326 constituencies or more.

Who can and cannot vote

There are rules about who can and cannot vote in the UK.

Who can vote

✓ People aged 18 years or over on polling day who are:

- a UK or qualifying Commonwealth citizen
- registered to vote on the electoral register
- resident at an address in the UK (or a UK citizen living abroad who has been registered to vote in the UK in the last 15 years)
- homeless people who have completed a declaration of local connection form
- not legally excluded from voting.

✓ Candidates standing in the election.

✓ Members of Parliament.

Who cannot vote

- Members of the House of Lords (a condition of their position).
- Economic migrants from the European Union who do not have full UK citizenship.
- Convicted prisoners.
- Persons found guilty of election corruption (barred for five years).

Debates around extending the franchise

The most common debate about extending the franchise (right to vote) is in relation to those aged between 16 and 18.

👍 **Those in favour** argue they should have a say in their future as a government is elected for five years and their education and training are directly affected by the policy makers; that they are allowed to do other responsible things at 16 such as choose their own medical treatment; and they may be more mature and educated than previous generations.

👎 **Those against** argue that some 16-year-olds are not well-informed, or are too immature to vote; that they might be influenced by peers or parents; and that the legally recognised age to be an adult is 18.

Now try this

Explain **two** reasons why some people may be reluctant to allow people aged 16 to vote in general elections.

(4)

Voting systems

The **first-past-the-post** electoral voting system used in UK general and local elections has strengths and weaknesses when compared with the **proportional representation** system.

First Past the Post (FPTP)

Here are **three** key points about FPTP:

1. The UK is divided into 650 constituencies (electoral areas). Each elects one candidate to become a Member of Parliament (MP).

2. Candidates standing in each constituency are listed on a ballot paper with the party they represent. Voters put a cross next to the candidate they want to vote for.

3. The candidate with the most votes is elected as MP for that constituency.

Strengths of the FPTP voting system	Weaknesses of the FPTP voting system
👍 It is a simple system to understand and doesn't cost much to run.	👎 Only winning votes count, so candidates may be elected on little public support.
👍 Results are calculated quickly and announced hours after voting has closed.	👎 It encourages tactical voting if a voter's preferred candidate is unlikely to win.
👍 It tends to produce a two-party system, resulting in single party governments.	👎 Some constituencies are 'safe seats', leading to voter apathy and reduced turnout.

Proportional representation (PR)

Here are **three** key points about the proportional representation system:

1. Seats are awarded depending on the percentage of votes each party wins.

2. Parties have a list of prospective candidates.

3. Candidates are allocated seats based on their popularity in the party.

Smaller parties argue for a voting system that more fairly represents the electorate's views. The table below shows the 2015 election results with FPTP and if a PR system had been used.

Party	% of Vote	Seats won	Seats if a PR system
Conservative	36.9%	331	239
Labour	30.4%	232	197
UKIP	12.6%	1	81
Liberal Democrat	7.9%	8	52
Scottish National Party	4.7%	56	30
Green Party	3.8%	1	24

Strengths of proportional representation	Weaknesses of proportional representation
👍 Fewer wasted votes.	👎 Produces more coalition governments.
👍 Offers more choice to voters.	👎 MPs may have no links to a constituency.
👍 Fairer to minority/independent candidates.	👎 Allows extremists in the political mainstream.

Now try this

Explain **two** criticisms that can be made of the first-past-the-post electoral system.   **(4)**

Forming a government

Following an election, the process of forming a single party or coalition government begins. The monarch appoints the Prime Minister and reads a speech in the State opening of Parliament.

Forming a single-party government

A party can form a single-party government if it has a **majority**.

- A majority is formed by winning **over half** the results in an election (326 or more of 650 seats).

- A majority is essential for Parliament to work, as each new law proposed by government needs to be voted on. If there is no majority, the opposition MPs could vote out proposed laws.

Forming a coalition government

If a party does not win a majority it is known as a **hung parliament**.

- The party with the most seats may form a coalition government with the support of another political party.

- Coalition government can mean it is more difficult to pass laws, as party values might need to be compromised to agree with coalition partners and vote laws through.

Confidence and supply agreement

Instead of forming a coalition government, a 'confidence and supply' agreement can be made with another party to support the government on a vote-by-vote basis.

Role of the monarch

There are **two** key roles for the monarch in forming a new government.

1. **Appointing the government**. The monarch meets the leader of the winning party. After the leader confirms they can form a new government, the monarch appoints them as Prime Minister.

2. **Reading the speech at the State opening of Parliament**. The monarch reads a speech in the House of Lords to officially open the new sitting of Parliament. This is written by the new government and outlines their policies and proposed legislation.

The monarch appoints Black Rod, whose role includes responsibility for major ceremonial events. After the monarch has read the speech and left, Parliament starts debating the issues in the speech.

Black Rod's ceremonial role

The tradition of the State opening of Parliament goes back to the 14th century.

- It takes place in the House of Lords, which consists of about 800 unelected peers from a mixture of backgrounds.

- Black Rod, a senior officer in the House of Lords, summons the House of Commons which consists of 650 elected Members of Parliament, to hear the speech.

- The doors of the House of Commons are first shut in Black Rod's face as a symbol of independence from the monarchy, a tradition from the Civil War.

- After Black Rod strikes the door three times it is opened, and the MPs follow Black Rod to the House of Lords to hear the speech.

Forming a cabinet

The Prime Minister then has a duty to appoint around 22 trusted party members, known as the **cabinet**, to develop policies and lead departments.

Now try this

Explain **two** reasons why a party would prefer to form a majority government. (4)

Organisation of a government

The work of government requires organisation into administrative departments, ministries and agencies, staffed by civil servants.

Differences between government ministers and civil servants

Government ministers	Civil servants
Elected politicians	Appointed officials
Represent a political party	Politically neutral
Can be changed through election or cabinet reshuffle	Permanent
Responsible to Parliament	Responsible to ministers
Head of a ministerial department	Work in ministerial departments
Decide policies to implement	Prepare and advise on policy

Ministerial departments

The new Prime Minister appoints cabinet ministers from the House of Commons and the House of Lords who are each given responsibility for a government department. The number of departments can change depending on the needs of the country at the time. Key departments include:

- Department for Education
- The Home Office
- Her Majesty's Treasury
- Ministry of Defence.

Senior civil servants

There are around 4,000 senior civil servants who work with government departments in a non-political role. Their jobs are permanent and not affected by the outcome of elections. Senior civil servants:

- undertake the preparation and presentation of new policies and are experts in their particular area
- often advise ministers, especially those newly appointed, on policies ministers wish to present in government.

Senior Civil Service roles

Day to day a senior civil servant will:

- prepare legislation
- find the answers to parliamentary questions
- brief their government minister
- manage the policies as they progress through the law-making procedure
- meet with representatives of different groups.

Civil servants

Civil servants are accountable to relevant ministers and strive to uphold values such as:

- **Integrity** – putting the needs of the public above personal interests.
- **Honesty** – they are subjected to public scrutiny so have to be open and honest.
- **Objectivity** – making decisions after evaluating all the relevant evidence.
- **Impartiality** – serving all governments equally well.

Civil Service roles

Over 400,000 other civil servants work across the UK. These civil servants administer government funds, institutions and departments, such as: paying benefits and pensions, running local departments such as Jobcentre Plus, running Her Majesty's Prison Service, administration, for example, driving license applications.

Now try this

Explain **two** duties of a senior civil servant in Westminster. (4)

Westminster Parliament

The **executive**, the **legislature**, the **judiciary** and the **monarchy** all have distinct roles in the Westminster Parliament. This **separation of powers** exists to protect citizens, and ensure that no one government or leader has too much power.

Separation of powers

The separation of powers into **four** distinct roles is also known as a system of checks and balances. In theory, the parts of the separation of power should be independent. In the UK system, there is an overlap between the executive and the legislature.

① **The executive: the Prime Minister and Cabinet propose new laws**

The Prime Minster and Cabinet draw up and propose the majority of new laws, with the help of the Civil Service. Being in the majority in government means they have the numbers to vote laws through in the House of Commons.

② **The legislature: the Houses of Commons and Lords make and change the law**

Westminster is **bicameral**, meaning it is a political system of **two houses** that make up the legislature. The members of both houses debate, scrutinise, vote, and create special committees to amend bills before they can be passed as laws. This means that new laws **cannot** be passed that would solely benefit the government in power, such as changing elections to every 25 years. The House of Lords can also act as an effective opposition at times when a majority government is strong and the opposition is perceived as weak.

③ **The judiciary: judges and magistrates apply the law**

Judges and magistrates in courts interpret the laws and apply appropriate sentences for criminal behaviour in line with existing laws.

④ **The monarchy: is integral to process and gives Royal Assent to each law**

Although the monarch no longer rules the country, the monarchy is integral to the law-making process and traditions of parliament. The role of the monarchy in parliament is to remain politically neutral, give Royal Assent to each new law and appoint Black Rod (senior officer in House of Lords, see page 27). After a general election, the monarch appoints the Prime Minister and opens each new session of Parliament.

Private Members' Bills

The executive does not propose all new laws. Private Members' Bills are introduced by members of the House of Lords or the House of Commons who are not members of the government. They can be introduced in either House and go through the same law-making stages. However, if unsupported by government, they are unlikely to become law.

Now try this

Explain **two** roles of the judiciary in the UK.   (4)

Houses of Commons and Lords

The business of Parliament takes place in the **House of Commons** and the **House of Lords**.

Relationship between the houses

The work of both houses is to make laws, check the work of government, hold parliamentary debates and deliberate on public issues as part of the process of making and shaping policy and legislation. Generally, decisions made in one House have to be approved by the other House, creating a system of checks and balances. The work of government is recorded in Hansard, a transcription of debates and speeches in both Houses. This is the official record, so can be scrutinised by the general public and journalists.

House of Commons

The House of Commons is the **publicly elected** House of Parliament.

The House of Commons consists of 650 Members of Parliament, each elected to represent their constituency (area) of the UK.

Role of the House of Commons

Main roles include:

- debating, examining, proposing and passing laws (see page 32).

- working in small (**select**) committees scrutinising new laws and wider areas of government work, to challenge and hold government to account.

- making decisions on financial bills, such as proposed new taxes. The House of Lords can consider these bills but cannot block or amend them.

- preparing questions to be answered at Prime Minister's Question Time.

House of Lords

The House of Lords is the **unelected** House of Parliament, also known as the 'second chamber'. It is independent from the House of Commons.

The House of Lords consists of about 800 peers from a mix of backgrounds, for example, hereditary and lifetime peers, bishops, judges, retired MPs, and people appointed due to personal experience. Some peers have party allegiances while others are crossbenchers and are not affiliated to any party. The House of Lords is also known as a 'revising chamber' for its role and expertise when scrutinising bills passed by the House of Commons.

Role of the House of Lords

Main roles include:

- debating, examining, proposing and passing laws (see page 32).

- working in small (**select**) committees to scrutinise and amend new laws and bills proposed by the House of Commons, and using their expertise to identify any errors.

- providing expertise in specific areas.

Now try this

Explain **two** roles of the House of Commons.　　　　(4)

The role of ministers and MPs

The work of the Parliament at Westminster involves many roles and responsibilities. Here are some key examples. You can revise the role and responsibilities of **Black Rod** on page 28.

The Prime Minister

The Prime Minister is an MP who is appointed by the monarch to lead the government (see page 27). The Prime Minister (PM) has the following roles and responsibilities:

* leadership of the country
* leadership of the party
* setting policy in line with their manifesto
* management and leadership of Cabinet ministers
* overseeing government and the Civil Service
* First Lord of the Treasury
* answering minister's questions during PM's Question Time.

Cabinet ministers

Cabinet ministers are selected by the Prime Minister (see page 27). They have **four** key roles:

1. making decisions about national issues
2. directing government policy
3. running governmental departments supported by senior civil servants (see page 28)
4. proposing new laws (see page 29).

Opposition and Shadow Cabinet ministers

The leader of the second largest party in the House of Commons leads the official **opposition**.

* The opposition leader selects a **Shadow Cabinet** to mirror the roles of the Cabinet.
* It holds Cabinet ministers to account through scrutiny of their work.
* It develops policies in specific areas and may block or undermine government policy.
* If the opposition wins the next election, shadow ministers often take Cabinet positions.

MP roles

MPs have **three** main areas of responsibility.

1. **Party responsibilities** include promoting the party's manifesto, voting in support of party policies and behaving in line with party guidelines.

2. **Commons responsibilities** include sitting on committees, participating in debates, voting on legislation and representing their constituency.

3. **Constituency responsibilities** include running surgeries, representing constituents' interests, attending local events, advocating local causes, supporting constituents with personal issues such as housing requirements, and writing letters of support.

MP positions

MPs may also have ministerial or shadow positions.

* **Front-bench MPs** are those with ministerial positions who are spokespeople for their party, so sit at the front.
* **Back-bench MPs** do not have a shadow or ministerial position, so sit on benches behind the front benchers.
* **Whips** are MPs appointed to organise party members, with a key responsibility to ensure MPs vote in line with party views.
* The **Speaker of the House of Commons** is an MP elected in Parliament to keep order, call MPs to speak, chair debates, suspend the House if serious disorder breaks out, and suspend MPs if they disobey House rules.

Now try this

Explain **two** roles of the Speaker of the House of Commons.   (4)

Making and shaping law

Bills become law through debate in the House of Commons and the House of Lords, scrutiny by committees, and Royal Assent. New laws in the UK may be:

(1) proposed by the government in power, as presented in their election **manifesto**. They have a **mandate** (authority) to implement them, with voters' support.

(2) prompted by current events, for example, new technology, acts of terror or environmental issues.

(3) prompted by issues covered in the media or through the work of **pressure groups**. Pressure groups are groups of people seeking to influence government policy or legislation.

The law-making process

A bill becomes law through debate in the House of Commons and the House of Lords, scrutiny by committees and Royal Assent by the monarch. The process is outlined below.

Green Paper – Consultation stage		The proposed law from the House of Commons or Lords is discussed with experts, interested groups and senior civil servants to inform and shape the proposal.
White Paper		This is the bill that will be presented to the houses, prepared after Green Paper consultation.
HOUSE OF COMMONS		**HOUSE OF LORDS**
First Reading – the bill is presented to the House and made available to its members.	**Parliamentary ping-pong** – the bill may go back and forth between the Houses until both the Commons and the Lords agree.	**First Reading** – the bill is presented to the House and made available to its members.
Second Reading – the bill is debated in the House – MPs may vote on the bill at this stage.		**Second Reading** – the bill is debated in the House. No vote is taken.
Committee Stage – a committee is formed of about 20 MPs to scrutinise the bill and vote on suggested amendments.		**Committee Stage** – usually the whole House will scrutinise the bill and propose amendments.
Report Stage – the amended bill is presented to the House; those not involved at committee stage may propose changes.		**Report Stage** – the amended bill is presented to the House; those not involved at committee stage may propose changes.
Third Reading – MPs vote on the fully amended bill.		**Third Reading** – the Lords may still introduce new amendments.
Royal Assent		After the Lords and Commons agree the bill, it is formally approved by the monarch. This is called **Royal Assent**, which turns the bill into legislation (law) when it becomes an **Act of Parliament**.

Now try this

New laws are usually proposed by governments. Suggest two reasons why a government may wish to make a new law.   (2)

The British Constitution

Democracy in the UK works through the **three** institutions of the British Constitution.

The House of Commons debates bills and passes laws.

The House of Lords scrutinises and amends bills.

The Monarch, as Head of State, formally approves new laws.

The British Constitution

The British Constitution defines the laws and political principles of the UK, and clarifies the relationship between citizens and the political state. The key principle is of **parliamentary sovereignty**, which states that Parliament is the legal authority that can make and change laws. The constitution consists of:

* **laws** and **legislation** passed by parliament
* **conventions** developed over time
* **common law** or **case law** developed and decided by judges.

Features of the British Constitution

The institutions that make up the British Constitution have many functions within them:

* the power of government and the role of the opposition
* the power of the Prime Minister, Cabinet, and role of the Civil Service (pages 27–31)
* the roles of the legislature and the judiciary (page 29) and of the police
* the role of citizens, political parties and the monarch (pages 22–31)
* the uncodified constitution (page 34)
* parliamentary sovereignty (page 35).

The power of government

The government is the basis of power in the constitution, as it forms the main source of new legislation.

* Power is derived from a majority of seats held in the House of Commons, which comes from the electorate who voted for the government. Governments with large majorities have more power to pass legislation.
* The Prime Minister and the Cabinet are the most powerful in deciding the direction of new legislation and the work of individual government departments, with support of the experts in the Civil Service.
* The political authority of the state is divided into legislative, executive and judicial powers to ensure that laws are applied consistently and fairly to UK citizens (see page 29).

The role of the opposition

The opposition is made up of those MPs from all political parties that are not in power (see page 31). The opposition:

* are a credible alternative to a current government in elections
* monitors the work of government and challenges their policies
* can make a government reverse unpopular policies
* can suggest amendments to bills proposed by government
* can voice the public's views and concerns.

Now try this

Suggest **three** reasons why it is important for democracy in the UK that there is an official opposition to a government.

(3)

Uncodified constitution

The UK has an uncodified constitution which has evolved over hundreds of years. Recent changes include the result of devolution, and the UK's relationship with the EU.

Uncodified constitution

The UK Constitution is uncodified, which means it is from a **number of sources** and has not been formally written down in one document. It reflects hundreds of years of laws from the four UK nations. There are **four** main sources of the British Constitution:

1. **Legislation** – laws passed by parliament, for example, statute law such as devolution.

2. **Conventions** – practices which have developed over time and regulate how government is run, for example, the Ministerial Code.

3. **Common law** or **case law** – when judges set precedent during court cases on how law should be interpreted and applied.

Codified constitution

A codified constitution is a **single document** which outlines the way in which a political state is governed. There are **three** main principles of a codified constitution:

1. It is **authoritative** – it defines the way that political institutions, including the legislature, operate.

2. It is **entrenched** – it is extremely difficult to amend or rescind a codified constitution.

3. It is **judiciable** – as it is a higher law that new laws have to be judged against, therefore it is judiciable, interpreted by and applied by the judiciary.

Advantages and disadvantages of an uncodified constitution

Advantages	Disadvantages
👍 It is flexible, allowing each new government to change legislation.	👎 Citizens may not clearly understand the constitution.
👍 Constitutional changes, such as devolution, can be made.	👎 It may be easier for controversial laws to be passed, or unpopular actions taken, such as the Iraq War.
👍 Urgent legislation can be passed quickly in response to new issues in society. Laws can be implemented that reflect changes in attitudes in society, for example, the Equality Act 2010.	👎 Laws being subject to change could affect the rights citizens are entitled to, for example, the idea of a British Bill of Rights versus the Human Rights Act.

Examples of how the uncodified constitution is changing

The impact of **devolution** is a good example of how an uncodified constitution can bring about major political change:

- **Devolution** – Wales, Scotland and Northern Ireland now have the right to legislate on devolved issues in each country, and each has its own assembly. Westminster Parliament can only legislate on reserved and excepted matters, and matters that only concern England.

Now try this

Name **three** sources of the uncodified constitution in the UK.   (3)

Parliamentary sovereignty

The constitutional concept of parliamentary sovereignty states that Parliament is the supreme body that creates or abolishes laws, and cannot be overruled. Parliament holds the government to account through oversight and scrutiny. Checks and balances include judicial review.

Parliamentary sovereignty

Parliamentary sovereignty is the most important part of the UK constitution.

* It makes Parliament the supreme legal authority in the UK.
* Future Parliaments can make their own laws and amend or remove any existing laws.
* The government must be drawn from Members of Parliament.
* Parliament is held to account through oversight, scrutiny, and a system of checks and balances, operating within the separation of powers (see page 29).

The European Union

Some argue that belonging to the European Union infringed on parliamentary sovereignty, as the European Communities Act 1972 gives priority to EU law over the laws of its member states.

The role of judicial review

Judicial review is a type of court proceeding. A judge reviews the lawfulness of decisions or actions taken by a public body, usually in central or local government. If the court finds a decision unlawful it can impose injunctions on the public body and may award damages.

Reasons for reversing decisions through judicial review include the following:

* **Ultra vires** – decisions made beyond the legal power or authority of the decision-maker, resulting in errors in applying the law.
* **Irrationality** (unreasonableness) – if the decision defies logic or acceptable moral standards.
* **Procedural impropriety** – if proper legal processes have not been followed.
* **Legitimate expectation** – if the person believed the promises or policies of a public body that were not adhered to.

Select committees

Select committees operate in both the House of Commons and the House of Lords. Their role is to check and report back on the work of government departments. The public can follow their findings by reading reports published by Parliament. Government has to respond to issues raised by select committees.

* The **House of Lords** select committees focus on the EU, science and technology, communications, the constitution, economic affairs and international relations.
* The **House of Commons** select committees examine the work of government department spending, policies and administration, current issues, or allegations of improper behaviour made against individual MPs.

Parliamentary inquiries

Parliamentary inquiries can be called to scrutinise the work of government in a specific area, if government are seen to be at fault. For example, after the 'Children of Windrush' scandal, in which some long-time immigrants from the Caribbean were threatened with deportation, an inquiry was started to investigate and suggest reforms. Recommendations included parliamentary apologies, compensation and the removal of a net migration target that might encourage the Home Office to deport more people without sufficient checks.

Now try this

Explain the meaning of the concept of 'parliamentary sovereignty'. (2)

Devolution in the UK

Devolution in the UK is the delegation of powers from the central government at Westminster to a national level following referendums held in Wales (1997), Scotland (1997) and Northern Ireland (1998). This led to the creation of the Welsh Assembly (1999), the Scottish Parliament (1999) and the Northern Ireland Assembly (1998) as part of the Good Friday agreement.

Devolution

The extent to which powers are devolved reflects the strength of the referendum vote.

The key argument for devolution is that:

• a local parliament or national assembly can better represent the needs of their citizens.

• each country will have a measure of self-government within the UK.

The Westminster Parliament

Although devolution has taken place, the UK Parliament votes on the following **reserved matters** for the whole of the UK, as well as devolved issues for England.

Reserved matters that have not been devolved			
the constitution	financial/economic	aspects of transport	equal opportunities
foreign affairs	immigration	employment	broadcasting
defence	drug control	energy regulation	ethical and medical matters
the Civil Service	trade and industry	social security	international development

The Scottish Parliament

Scotland has a long history of independence and high local support for devolution. In the referendum, 74% voted 'yes'.

Scotland's devolved powers include	
environment	local government and housing
agriculture	health and social work
forestry	justice and policing
fishing	economic development
education	tourism, sport and heritage

Scottish elections

Voters in Scottish Parliament elections have two votes to elect the 129 Members of Sottish Parliament (MSPs).

• The first vote is to elect a candidate using FPTP. One MSP represents each of the 73 constituencies.

• 56 MSPs are then elected using a system of proportional representation. Voters choose a party or independent candidate for their region. Seven MSPs represent each of the 8 regions.

The Welsh Assembly

The Welsh Assembly originally held fewer devolved powers as it is a smaller country than Scotland with less history of self-governance. The referendum was close, with 50.03% voting 'yes'. Welsh devolved powers are now similar to Scotland's, without justice and policing but including promotion of the Welsh language.

The Northern Ireland Assembly

Northern Ireland's devolved powers are similar to Scotland's but they can vote on some reserved matters with agreement of the Secretary of State. In periods of Assembly suspension due to political disagreement, decisions revert to Westminster.

English votes for English laws

Following devolution, a process was introduced to ensure that legislation that affects only England is approved by a majority of MPs representing English constituencies.

Now try this

Name **two** devolved powers of Scotland.   (2)

Changing relations

The relationships between England, Scotland, Wales and Northern Ireland are changing, including views on devolution and independence.

Scottish independence

Devolution has prompted calls for Scottish independence, and a referendum was taken in 2014, which extended the voting franchise to 16-year-olds. The outcome of the vote was to stay, with 55.3% voting not to leave. Following the UK's referendum to leave the EU, there have been further calls for independence as a majority of voters in Scotland (62%) voted to remain in the EU.

Arguments for and against Scottish independence in 2014

For independence	Against independence
Decisions about Scotland should be made by Scottish citizens.	The UK has won wars, built an empire, and been a successful union for 300 years.
Scottish taxation and spending would make them a more successful country.	Being part of the UK means being part of the EU and single market.
Scotland could focus on Scottish issues and priorities.	Businesses could move their established bases to somewhere else in the UK, leading to a loss of Scottish jobs due to new taxes and regulations.
Scotland would not have to fight British wars or be home to Trident.	Scotland would need to establish a currency union to continue to use the pound.
Scotland has an ageing population and could more easily encourage economic migrants.	The UK is an influential member of international organisations like NATO and the UN. Scotland would be less influential.
Scotland could still have a good relationship with the UK but on an equal footing.	Joint security across the UK is better.

Wales

After the initial establishment of the Welsh Assembly in 1998, power devolved further.

- In 2010, the Assembly organised a referendum for further legislative powers for Wales.
- In 2011, Wales was given new powers to legislate for all 20 devolved areas for Wales.
- Devolved areas include culture, the Welsh language and ancient monuments, all of which strengthen the Welsh national identity. For example, the Welsh Language Measure 2011 allows ministers to impose standards on organisations not treating Welsh and English equally.

Northern Ireland

Since its creation, The Northern Ireland Assembly has had five periods of suspension, when relations between the different parties in Northern Ireland have been strained. During times of suspension, power to legislate in Northern Ireland reverts to Westminster.

Now try this

Explain **one** way that devolution has strengthened the Welsh national identity.   (4)

Brexit

Brexit may bring about further changing relations.

Direct and indirect taxes

Central government raises funds through direct and indirect taxes in order to finance public services such as education, the National Health Service, and defence.

Direct taxes

Direct taxation describes taxes paid by a person or organisation, which cannot be passed to anyone else or ignored. Examples of direct tax in the UK include:

- **Income tax:** tax on your wages when you earn above a certain amount.
- **Inheritance tax:** tax on money left to you in a will when someone has died.
- **Corporation tax:** a percentage tax based on the profits a business makes.
- **National Insurance contributions:** a form of taxation based on income, originally to fund the welfare state. Contributions made when working now fund state pensions.
- **Council tax:** a tax paid annually based on the value of the property that you live in, collected by the local authority.

Indirect taxes

Indirect taxation describes taxes paid on goods and services. Examples of indirect taxes in the UK include:

- **VAT (value added tax):** a tax on most things you buy in the UK, currently charged at a rate of 20% on most goods and services. Some items are VAT free, for example, children's clothes.
- **Excise duties:** tax levied on items such as alcohol or tobacco.

Use of indirect taxes

Indirect taxes can have **advantages** as they are cheaper to collect, penalise spending rather than success, and can discourage spending on items harmful to health which can cost tax-payer's money through the NHS.

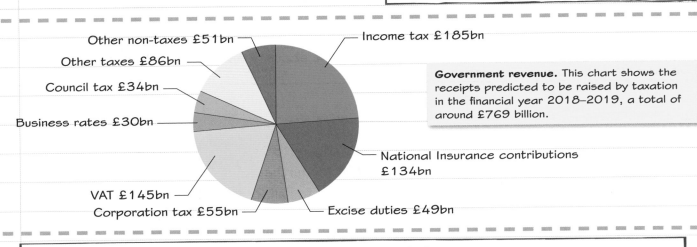

Other non-taxes £51bn
Other taxes £86bn
Council tax £34bn
Business rates £30bn
VAT £145bn
Corporation tax £55bn
Income tax £185bn
National Insurance contributions £134bn
Excise duties £49bn

Government revenue. This chart shows the receipts predicted to be raised by taxation in the financial year 2018–2019, a total of around £769 billion.

Her Majesty's Revenue and Customs (HMRC)

HMRC is a non-ministerial governmental department. It is responsible for:

- the collection of taxation
- the payment of some types of state support
- administration of some regulations such as the national minimum wage
- investigating smuggling, fraud and tax evasion as a law enforcement agency, where punishment for tax evasion can be imprisonment.

Now try this

Name **three** direct taxes in the UK. (3)

The Chancellor of the Exchequer

The role of the Chancellor of the Exchequer is to budget for income, expenditure and debts, manage risks, and make decisions about the allocation of public funding.

The Chancellor of the Exchequer

The Chancellor of the Exchequer is the government's chief financial minister, and is one of the most important roles in the Cabinet. The key responsibilities of the role are:

- raising revenue for the government through taxation or borrowing.
- controlling how government revenue is spent.
- leading the Treasury, a ministerial department made up of junior ministers and civil servants.
- allocating the expenditure limits for all other government departments.

The budget

A key aspect of the Chancellor's role is to allocate the annual budget for government spending on public services.

- Traditionally, the budget was delivered in March as the financial year starts in April. In 2018, the annual budget was delivered in October.
- The budget speech is delivered in the House of Commons and is carried in a red briefcase.
- A review of the budget happens six months after it is delivered. This looks at the spending for the next financial year.

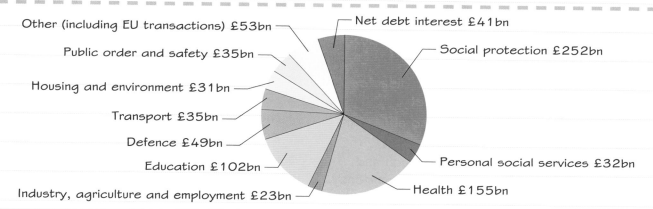

Other (including EU transactions) £53bn
Public order and safety £35bn
Housing and environment £31bn
Transport £35bn
Defence £49bn
Education £102bn
Industry, agriculture and employment £23bn
Net debt interest £41bn
Social protection £252bn
Personal social services £32bn
Health £155bn

Public sector spending. This chart shows predicted spending on public services for the financial year 2018-2019, a total of £809 billion. This exceeds the income predicted of £769 billion (see page 38). When a government cannot raise enough money through taxation it needs to borrow money. The role of the Chancellor is to balance the books.

Managing allocation of public funding

When government income is less than government expenditure, as with the £40bn difference between the income shown on page 39 and the expenditure shown above, the Chancellor has to manage risks and make decisions about the allocation of public funding. This can lead to a period of austerity in government spending.

Austerity

Austerity is an economic term to describe how a government will try to reduce its budget deficits (the amount it needs to balance spending and income). Common ways to reduce the deficit are to increase taxation and to reduce spending through budget cuts.

Now try this

Explain, giving an example, **one** responsibility of the Chancellor of the Exchequer. **(2)**

Budget and provision

There are many different views and debates about how governments and other service providers make provision for welfare, health, the care of the elderly, and education.

Budget provision and priorities

Each political party has ideas on how much provision should be made by government, and how much citizens should provide themselves.

- Prior to each election, the political parties identify their budgetary plans should they win the election.
- Some parties would tax the rich, some would increase VAT, and some would cut government spending.
- Most governments agree on the importance of defence spending, with some debate about spending on nuclear weapons.

Health

The National Health Service (NHS) offers free health care for citizens but increased demand is putting it under pressure. Key debates include whether:

- people who can afford private healthcare should pay for services
- people with self-inflicted illnesses should help themselves
- wider solutions can be found for adult social care and an ageing population
- the NHS should remain free as the public demand, with increased funding.

Welfare

Government provides benefits for those who cannot find work or are unfit to work. Key debates **for** and **against** welfare include:

- 👍 Benefits provide a safety net.
- 👍 Fit people need to look after disabled, elderly and ill people in society.
- 👎 The benefit system is open to abuse and some commit benefit fraud.
- 👎 Some think benefits cost too much and create a cycle of poverty and dependency. However, more is spent on pensions and those not paid appropriately.

Education

Education is important, as a well-educated population provides the innovation and entrepreneurial skills of the future workforce. Key debates include:

- impacts of cutting the budget, increasing class sizes, and limiting school resources
- the cost of university may be deterring poorer people from studying for a degree
- students who can afford to go to private school often have better outcomes
- grammar schools create a selective system, often based on parental resources.

Care of the elderly

With an increasingly ageing population, key debates include:

- taking personal responsibility for old age through savings and pensions
- families caring for elderly relatives
- increasing tax to cover increased costs
- considering new ways the NHS and care in the community can work together.

Charities

A key debate concerns how far citizens can work themselves out of poverty and the role of charities with vulnerable citizens through:

- homeless shelters and soup kitchens
- food banks for those living in poverty
- phone support for the aged and those with mental health issues
- free legal advice and debt guidance.

Now try this

Suggest **two** possible reasons why a government might decide to increase spending on the NHS. (2)

Short answer questions

In **Paper 1, Section B**, questions are focused on **Theme B: Democracy at work in the UK.**

Paper 1 Section B short answer questions

Short answer questions require you to demonstrate your knowledge and understanding of citizenship concepts, terms and issues. Here are command words you might see:

- **which, give, identify, name**: you need to give a point or example without further development.
- **explain**: you need to make a point and then develop it to show your understanding.
- **suggest**: you need to show your understanding when reasons are less clear cut.

Worked example

Identify **one** reason why a coalition government might be formed after an election. **(1)**

If no single party has a working majority.

Explain **two** differences between the Labour and Liberal Democrat party philosophies. **(4)**

1 The Liberal Democrats are more libertarian than Labour. They are more committed to individual freedom, while Labour supports more government intervention.

2 Labour favour raising higher tax rates to pay for services. This is because they claim to be the party of working people, whereas the Liberal Democrats say they are not as closely linked to any social class.

Which of these formally appoints Black Rod? **(1)**

☒ A The monarch
☐ B The House of Commons
☐ C The House of Lords
☐ D The Speaker

Name **one** stage that a bill has to go through in the House of Commons before it receives Royal Assent. **(1)**

Report stage.

Which of these is **not** a job of the Chancellor of the Exchequer? **(1)**

☐ A Arranging government borrowing
☐ B Reviewing departmental spending plans
☒ C Deciding when to raise interest rates
☐ D Introducing new taxes

Suggest **one** advantage for the government of using indirect taxation rather than direct taxation. **(1)**

Indirect taxes are cheaper to collect.

This needs one simple point without development.

Party philosophies are about the principles members support, not specific details that may change with each election. You need to make an initial point and then develop the details of your explanation to show your understanding. Don't just write about one of the parties. You must compare them to show the differences.

The role is a senior officer in the House of Lords with responsibility for major ceremonial events, and is officially appointed by the monarch.

'Name' questions test recall of knowledge and do not need development.

Interest rates (C) are controlled by the Bank of England.

Now try this

Explain **two** advantages of having the House of Lords as a 'revising chamber'.

Show you understand the term 'revising chamber' (see page 30).

Had a look ☐　Nearly there ☐　Nailed it! ☐

Source B questions 1

In **Paper 1, Section B**, you will need to apply knowledge and understanding of citizenship concepts, terms and issues to contexts and actions as you respond to a source.

Paper 1 Section B Source B questions

One question in **Section B: Democracy at work in the UK** is based on Source B. You will need to read the source and then answer a question about it. Here are command words you might see:

- **explain:** you need to provide a reasoned explanation that shows your understanding through justifying or giving examples of the points you have identified, applied to a source.

- **compare:** you need to compare two or more issues, opinions or situations.

Source B

Study Source B and then answer the question on the next page.

Source B: 2010 and 2017 election results

Party	2010	2017
Conservative	306	318
Labour	258	262
Liberal Democrat	57	12
Scottish Nationalist Party (SNP)	6	35
Democratic Unionist Party (DUP)	8	10
Sinn Fein	5	7
Others	10	6

650 MPs. Majority required is 326.

In the 2010 election, <u>no party had a clear majority</u> of 326 MPs needed to form a government. The Prime Minister, Gordon Brown, resigned and was replaced by David Cameron as Conservative Prime Minister. <u>He set up a formal coalition government with the Liberal Democrats</u>. This was the UK's first coalition formed as a direct result of election results. A bonus for the Liberal Democrats was that it gave them government experience for the first time.

<u>The 2017 election resulted in a hung parliament. Instead of a formal alliance with any party Theresa May made an informal 'confidence and supply' agreement</u> with the Democratic Unionist Party (DUP). This meant the DUP would <u>support her minority government on a vote-by-vote basis.</u> There was <u>no formal written agreement.</u> In return, the government <u>pledged a billion pounds in extra funding for Northern Ireland</u> and Mrs May claimed there had been a long relationship between the two parties. Ulster Unionist MPs had supported John Major's minority government in 1996–1997.

Read the source carefully. It relates to the question on page 44, which is about explaining differences between a coalition and a minority government in the UK.

Underlining key points can help focus your answer. Here, for example, consider points relating to:

- the election results and what leaders would need to consider in response to them

- why Brown resigned (because he could not get support of all the minor parties for the 326 votes required)

- the small majority Theresa May had in 2017, and her miscalculation in holding an election, which meant that, for a commanding majority, she needed support of the DUP, who refused a formal agreement

- the implications of the confidence and supply agreement with the DUP.

Other minority governments had been formed after Assembly elections in 2007 for Wales and Scotland, as no party had a majority of seats in either country.

Now try this

The source refers to a 'confidence and supply' agreement. Explain what this means.

To revise 'confidence and supply', see page 27.

Source B questions 2

This response to an **explain** question relates to the source on page 43. It shows the qualities your answer to an 'explain' question should demonstrate:

- detailed knowledge about the concepts, terms and issues relevant to the question
- good understanding of how they apply by effective and sustained comment about the source context.

Worked example

Source B is about coalition and minority governments in the UK.
Use Source B and your own knowledge to explain differences between a coalition and a minority government in the UK.   **(6)**

Source B says the UK had a coalition government in 2010, and minority governments in 1996–1997 and 2017. The table shows that in 2010 and 2017 neither of the two largest parties had enough MPs to have a majority in Parliament (326 MPs), which is needed if the government is to get its laws passed.

In 2010, Labour were 68 seats short and the Conservatives, the largest party, needed another 20 votes. To get a majority Labour would have needed the support of all of the smaller parties (Sinn Fein MPs don't attend Parliament). Conservative leader Mr Cameron had a choice. He could ask some of the smaller parties to promise to support him, or he could make a formal agreement with the Liberal Democrats, the third largest party. He decided to make a formal written agreement, and so the Conservatives and Liberal Democrats formed a government between them. This is called a coalition.

A coalition government has a programme that both parties agree to support, and both parties have MPs in the cabinet. Coalitions are usually quite stable unless there is a major crisis. The 2010 coalition lasted throughout the life of the Parliament but the two parties split up for the election in 2015.

In 2017, Mrs May was eight MPs short of a majority. Her party could have tried to govern on its own, formed another coalition, or made an informal agreement with other parties. No other party was prepared to make a coalition. She decided to create a minority government after making an informal agreement with the DUP. They agreed to support the government on some important votes (but not necessarily all votes) in return for a billion pounds to be spent on Northern Ireland. The DUP were not members of the government.
A minority government is a lot less stable than a coalition because it is informal and can be easily broken if one party disagrees with the other.

This question asks you to relate to Source B (page 43) **and** your own knowledge in response. Westminster is not specified. You could write about minority governments in the Scottish Parliament or Welsh and Northern Ireland Assemblies.

Paragraphs 1 and 2 show understanding of the source, first identifying the key issue of hung parliaments and then going on to explain and interpret the importance of a majority, and the term 'coalition'.

Paragraphs 3 and 4 develop the explanation of differences and include own knowledge. The source is not simply repeated. This shows a detailed and sustained response. A conclusion is not required.

Now try this

Suggest why Theresa May did not form a coalition government after the 2017 election.   **(4)**

Practice short answer questions

Practise for **Paper 1, Section B,** with these exam-style short answer questions. Example answers are provided at the end of this book.

Guided

Identify **one** reason why the government has encouraged people
to save in a work-based pension scheme.   **(1)**

....

....

....

> Identify **one** reason. Development is not needed.

Explain **two** ways in which the separation of powers is necessary
to preserve democracy.   **(4)**
1 ....

....

....

2 ....

....

....

> Show you understand the meaning of 'separation of powers' as it applies to government (page 30). Explain two reasons that do not overlap. For each reason, make a point and then develop it. You could use an example in your development.

Which of these voting systems is used alongside the first-past-
the-post system in elections for the Scottish Assembly?   **(1)**
☐ **A** Alternative vote
☐ **B** Closed party lists vote
☐ **C** Additional member vote
☐ **D** The supplementary vote

> This is about the Assembly, not a method used for local elections.

Which **one** of these positions is elected by a vote of the
general public?   **(2)**
☐ **A** The Cabinet Secretary
☐ **B** The Lord Chief Justice
☐ **C** The Mayor of Greater Manchester
☐ **D** The Speaker of the House of Commons

> Read the multiple choice questions carefully and then mark the correct answer.

Name **one** role of the House of Commons.   **(1)**

....

....

....

> Give a short answer without development.

Suggest **one** reason why the Welsh Assembly has not been given
the same devolved powers as the Scottish Parliament.   **(1)**

....

....

....

> This question tests your understanding of devolution and your ability to surmise (to work things out from what you know).

Practice Source B questions

Practise for **Paper 1, Section B**, with this exam-style source question. Apply your knowledge and understanding of citizenship concepts, terms and issues in the context of the source. No conclusion is required. Example answers are provided at the end of this book.

Guided

Study Source B and then answer the question below.

Source B: How Italy makes laws

Italy's written constitution says that its Parliament, consisting of the Senate and the Chamber of Deputies, makes laws. Both chambers are equally involved in law-making. Both chambers must approve an identical text for a bill to become law. Law making is very slow. Any of Italy's regional councils can make their own laws, provided they 'do not affect the national state'.

A select parliamentary committee considers proposed laws and produces a revised text for MPs to discuss. Draft bills can go to either chamber first. Each political group can contribute to the debate. After proposed amendments are considered, an agreed final text is voted on.

The bill is then considered in the same way by the other chamber. Any revisions are sent to the first chamber for further review. This continues until full agreement is reached. The Italian President then must accept it or send it back for amendment. If agreed by both houses for a second time, the President must approve it. The new law is published, becoming effective 15 days later.

Source B is about the way that laws are made in Italy.

Using Source B and your own knowledge compare the way that laws are made in Italy with how they are made by the UK Parliament.

(6)

- Read the source and question carefully. You could underline relevant information in the source to help you focus your answer.
- You do not need to know more about the way laws are made in Italy than is in the source.

For a 'compare' question you should make sustained and effective comparisons between both contexts. Compare whether the UK has a written constitution, whether it has a two-chamber parliament, and whether there are regional assemblies.

You must show your own knowledge and understanding of UK law-making in comparison to the source information. Do not simply write out or summarise what the source says.

Compare whether both chambers in the UK make laws and whether or not they are equal, or which has greater authority.

Compare the revision process for UK laws and the role of the UK monarch concerning new laws.

There are a number of similarities and differences between both systems to examine.

Use a separate piece of paper to answer this question.

The role of law

The role of law is to provide a **set of rules** that all people in society must follow without exception, whether they are rich or poor, and whatever their status, origin or gender. This idea is called **the rule of law**, and is one of the key principles of a democratic society.

Keeping the law

Society has ideas about what types of behaviour are acceptable and unacceptable. Three key roles of the law are to:

1. **Set out what actions are acceptable** for people to carry out and what actions are not allowed, for example, stealing, assault, murder.

2. **Keep order in society** by providing a common understanding of what will happen if the law is not followed.

3. **Ensure fairness** so that everyone feels they get the outcome they deserve, and that no-one should be punished for something they did not do.

Maintaining order

Chaos and disorder may occur if criminal law is not strongly upheld, so laws are made to:

- **punish** those who break the law. Punishments include fines, imprisonment, or community service

- **deter** criminal behaviour, so people think about the consequences of their actions and avoid punishment, such as being sent to prison.

How the law affects our everyday lives

The law affects everything we do as citizens. It is not a matter of choice. It affects everyone. It helps society to deal with complex problems and tells us, for example:

- what we can own and buy
- where we can live
- what substances we can take into our bodies
- how we can be educated.

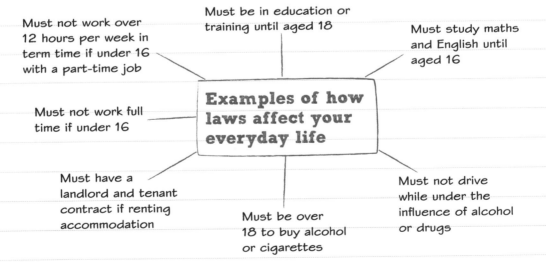

Must not work over 12 hours per week in term time if under 16 with a part-time job

Must be in education or training until aged 18

Must study maths and English until aged 16

Must not work full time if under 16

Examples of how laws affect your everyday life

Must have a landlord and tenant contract if renting accommodation

Must be over 18 to buy alcohol or cigarettes

Must not drive while under the influence of alcohol or drugs

Now try this

Suggest **three** ways that society might be different if there were no laws. (3)

Law in society

Laws are needed in society to protect the public, settle disputes, ensure that people are treated fairly (including preventing discrimination), change behaviour and respond to new situations in society, including scientific and technological developments and changing values.

Protecting the public

One of the key functions of the law is to protect the public. This links to the rights of citizens to live free from interference from others. Some important protections relate to the **right to be safe**, such as:

* protection from assault, injury, homicide (murder and manslaughter), burglary, and robbery
* health and safety protection in schools, homes, at work and in the community.

Settling disputes

Laws are used to settle disputes arising between people in society. This links with **civil law** and disputes relating to:

* marriages breaking down
* company disagreements about contracts
* neighbours disputing land boundaries
* consumer protection concerning items purchased from a supplier, such as a phone or television, through the Consumer Rights Act 2015.

Ensuring fair treatment

Laws such as the **Human Rights Act 1998** and the **Equality Act 2010** are in place to ensure people are treated fairly. This links to key values of equal opportunity and anti-discrimination. For example:

* **preventing discrimination** against people on grounds of ethnicity, age, gender, sexual orientation and disability
* **ensuring everyone has equal opportunities** to succeed, regardless of their personal characteristics.

Changing behaviour

The law can help change behaviour. For example:

* **deterrence** through punishment for behaviours such as stealing, to put people off
* **retribution** to a victim or to society, such as using community service to teach criminals their behaviour is wrong and to change their actions
* **rehabilitation** of a young person through education, training, or therapy, for example, removing the reason for offending.

Responding to new or changing situations

Law is also needed to respond to new situations in society. Here are **four** examples:

1. **Terrorism**, where groups such as ISIS emerge. The law must be dynamic and flexible to deal with it, keep the public safe, and uphold society's values.

2. **Scientific discoveries** that need to be regulated to reflect new developments. For example, the Human Fertilisation and Embryology Act 1991 prevents embryos being used for scientific experiments after 14 days. Some feel such experiments are unethical.

3. **New technologies** that emerge and need to be regulated, such as social media, where people's right to privacy may need protection. For example, Facebook harvested customers' data without their knowledge.

4. **Changes in values** held by society. For example, the Marriage (Same Sex Couples) Act 2013 reflects society's changing attitudes.

Now try this

Suggest **three** reasons why society needs laws.

(3)

Age of legal responsibility

The law sets out the age of criminal responsibility and the legal age limits that are designed to **protect** young people. These include the age they become legally responsible for actions such as driving, getting married, voting, working, and joining the armed forces.

Examples of legal age limits

Action	Age limit	Reason
Driving	17	Responsible enough to apply for a provisional driving licence, to take lessons, and drive a car
Getting married – with parental consent – without parental consent	16 18	Protects young people from pressure, abuse or exploitation by those who might try to take advantage of them, including older people
Voting	18	Responsible and independent enough to participate in the UK's democratic elections and referendums
Working – part time (with restrictions) – full time (with restrictions) – full time	13 16 18	Prevents unethical employers from exploiting children by making them work too many hours, affecting their education and health in a negative way
Joining the armed forces – with parental consent – without parental consent	16 18	Prevents decisions being made before reaching stages of maturity that occur in late adolescence, and acknowledges how interests and ambitions may change
Joining the navy	16	Responsible enough for an age-appropriate role (some roles restricted until aged 18)

Debates about legal age limits

Legal age limits are often debated. Here are **three** examples:

1. **Reduce the voting age from 18 to 16** as 16-year-olds are educated in citizenship, they can pay tax, marry, and join the navy. Sixteen-year-olds were also allowed to vote in the Scottish Referendum in 2014.

2. **Keep the voting age at 18** as 16-year-olds lack maturity and experience, may be easily influenced, and need parental permission to marry.

3. **Increase the age to join the armed forces from 16.** The UN Committee on Rights of the Child challenges the UK age limit of 16. In the USA, the minimum age is 17.

Age of criminal responsibility

The age of criminal responsibility in England and Wales is 10. In Scotland it is 8, although a bill in 2018 debated to increase it to age 12. In England and Wales:

- children under the age of 10 cannot be arrested or charged with a crime

- children aged 10 are considered old enough to understand the difference between right and wrong and are held responsible for the things they do

- young people from 10 to 17 can go to a youth court if charged with a crime

- those aged 18 can be sent to an adult court for trial.

Now try this

Explain, with **one** example, why there are legal limits on what a 16-year-old can do. (2)

Principles of law

The fundamental principles of law are to uphold citizen's rights and freedoms through the rule of law, the presumption of innocence, equality before the law, and equal access to justice.

Upholding rights and freedoms

All citizens have some basic rights and freedoms that governments must uphold, and the law protect. These include:

- the right to life
- the right to freedom of expression
- the right to a fair and free trial.

Rule of law

The rule of law includes **three** key points:

1. **all citizens must obey the law** and this applies equally to all, e.g. politicians, police, companies, monarchs, and ordinary citizens

2. **it protects citizens** against the abuse of power by their rulers (to revise the Magna Carta and the rule of law, see page 12)

3. **it ensures citizens are accountable** for their actions, as if anyone is found guilty of breaking the law they will be punished.

Presumption of innocence

The Magna Carta established a **right to a fair trial** with a presumption of **innocence**.

- When a person accused of an offence is taken to court, they are held to be innocent. The purpose of a trial is to hear evidence that might lead to conviction. The person on trial has a right to hear and defend themselves against this evidence.

- Until guilt is established beyond reasonable doubt, innocence is maintained.

Equality before the law

The rule of law results in all citizens in a democracy having a right:

- **to respect**, with no discrimination on grounds of their personal characteristics.
- **to a fair and public hearing** of their case with impartial juries and judges.
- **to prepare a defence** if accused, and to question witnesses as part of this.
- **for judgements** to be made **public.**
- **to appeal** against a decision all the way up to the highest court.

Access to justice

All citizens should have access to justice, with equality before the law and a fair trial.

- **No-one should suffer a miscarriage of justice** or unfair treatment due to social characteristics such as poverty.

- **A defendant (person on trial) has a right to a defence** and is entitled to legal representation in a police station and in court, which may be paid for through legal aid if needed.

Threats to access to justice

Here are **two** reasons why some feel access to justice could be better.

1. **Cuts to legal aid funding**: The Law Society has raised concerns that government cuts to legal aid are damaging access for poorer people.

2. **Closure of some local courts**: this means that people have to travel further to attend court which may be a burden on health or finances.

Now try this

Explain what is meant by 'the rule of law'.

(2)

Regional legal systems

The UK is a political union of four countries, and has more than one legal system. England and Wales share a legal system which is different from Scotland, and from Northern Ireland.

Different legal systems in the UK

There are historic reasons for the different legal systems in the UK, resulting in three separate **legal jurisdictions** (territories in which a particular legal system has authority).

1543: England and Wales joined together, sharing a system.

1707: Scotland joined England and Wales with the Act of Union to form Great Britain, but retained a separate system.

1801: Great Britain joined Ireland, which kept its courts.

1921: Most of Ireland became independent from Britain, though six counties in Northern Ireland remained but retained a different court system.

The three **legal jurisdictions** in the UK:
1) England and Wales
2) Scotland
3) Northern Ireland

England and Wales

England and Wales share legal jurisdiction.

- They share a common law legal system with criminal and civil law as parts of it. **Common law** refers to judge-made law, or case law. It stems from judges interpreting and referring to the law based on previous decisions. This is also known as **judicial precedent**.
- Wales also has an Assembly with some powers to make its own laws. It can amend UK laws to suit Wales, though it still shares legal jurisdiction with England.

The Welsh Assembly

The Welsh Assembly was set up in 1999 following a referendum (see page 36).

- It consists of 60 members.
- 40 are elected using the first-past-the-post system.
- 20 are topped up from party lists.
- It has responsibility for 20 devolved areas on which it can make its own laws, concerning matters such as education, health and housing.

Scotland

Scotland kept its own legal system which is based on **Roman law**.

- It practises Scots law, with a system that is largely separate from the rest of the UK.
- Areas such as employment law are similar.
- There are significant differences in property and criminal law. For example, in criminal trials juries have a third option of a 'not proven' verdict in addition to the 'guilty' or 'not guilty' verdicts of England and Wales.
- The UK Supreme Court is the highest court for appeals from Scottish citizens.

Northern Ireland

Northern Ireland (NI) has its own Assembly which can pass laws that are enforced by its own court system. It also has responsibility for education and planning in NI.

- The legal system of NI is based on common law, some of it coming from Irish common law before NI was part of the UK.
- It has laws passed by the UK Parliament.
- It has laws passed by the Parliament of Ireland prior to joining the UK in 1801.
- Not all UK laws apply in NI due to the country's historical and religious background. For example, the UK Abortion Act 1967 is not law in NI.

Now try this

Explain why one country in the UK does **not** use common law.   (2)

Sources of law

The main sources of law in the UK are **common law** (case law or precedent) and **legislation** made by Parliament. Also, the laws of the European Union (EU) when a member state.

Common law

Common law refers to laws made by judges in cases that have appeared before them.

- Much English law is common law and has **existed for a long time**.

- In medieval times judges would travel the country hearing cases and settling disputes. Their judgements became the **common law (or case law)** that could be referred to by other judges in similar cases.

- If a judge made a ruling on a case, it set a **precedent** for other judges to follow in future cases.

- **Common law** is still followed in the UK. Judges follow decisions made in the past by other judges of the same or superior rank.

New developments in technology might lead to **new precedents** being set. Judges need to interpret the law in light of developments such as social media and digital content. Judges can also recommend to Parliament that it brings the law up to date to reflect such changes.

Legislation

To 'make law' is to **legislate**. Parliament is the most important source of new legislation in the UK. Once a bill has passed through Parliament and become an Act, it is also known as a **statute**.

- The UK Parliament is sovereign, which means it can make law on anything it chooses.

- Most new laws start with the Government and have to be agreed to by Parliament.

- Many new laws start as proposals in the manifesto of the political party that wins the general election and forms the Government.

- Sometimes a new law can start with a Private Members' Bill. This is a process by which a backbench MP can propose some legislation on an issue they think is important or may be controversial.

- Only a few Private Members' Bills succeed because the Government takes up most of the time available in the House with debating new legislation it has developed.

Brexit and EU as a source of law

The UK joined the EU in 1973, and left in 2020. All laws of the EU must become part of the law of its members, and all laws passed in that country must be consistent with EU law. This situation means that some EU law, even after leaving the union, remains as a source of law in the UK. One of the key problems for the UK in leaving the EU is what should be done with the many laws that originated in the EU. Since the decision to leave the EU, Parliament has been deciding on the future of those laws.

Now try this

Identify **two** ways in which UK law is made.   (2)

Criminal and civil law

There are **two** types of law that protect citizens from crime or offences that are against the law. **Criminal law** maintains order and protects society as a whole. **Civil law** upholds the rights of individuals in disputes.

Criminal law

The purpose of criminal law is to protect the public from harm, such as in cases where crimes are committed against a **person** or **property**.

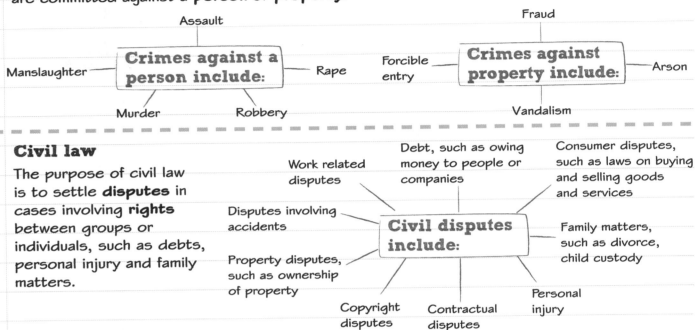

Assault

Crimes against a person include:

Manslaughter

Rape

Murder

Robbery

Forcible entry

Fraud

Crimes against property include:

Arson

Vandalism

Civil law

The purpose of civil law is to settle **disputes** in cases involving **rights** between groups or individuals, such as debts, personal injury and family matters.

Work related disputes

Debt, such as owing money to people or companies

Consumer disputes, such as laws on buying and selling goods and services

Disputes involving accidents

Civil disputes include:

Family matters, such as divorce, child custody

Property disputes, such as ownership of property

Copyright disputes

Contractual disputes

Personal injury

The different process in criminal and civil law

Process	Criminal law	Civil law
Courts where cases are heard	The state prosecutes alleged criminals in the **Magistrates' Court**, or the **Crown Court** for serious offences.	Cases are heard in the **County Court**, **High Court**, **Family Court** or by a **Tribunal**, depending on the type of case.
A case is brought against a defendant	Case is brought by the Crown Prosecution Service on behalf of the **state**, which acts for the community against the alleged criminal who has been accused of breaking the law.	Cases are brought by the **individual** or **business** affected by the dispute.
Burden of proof required	Is on the **prosecution** to prove the case.	Is on the **claimant** to show they have a case.
Standard of proof required	To be proved beyond a reasonable doubt.	The court or tribunal needs to be over 50% sure the defendant is liable.
Penalties	Include **imprisonment** (a custodial sentence), **fines** or **community service**.	Are **non-custodial** (not prison) such as winners getting **compensation** from losers, and losers paying the winner's **legal costs** as well as their own.

Now try this

Explain, using an example, what is meant by criminal law.   (2)

England and Wales justice system 1

The justice system in England and Wales involves the roles and powers of **police** and **judges** (revised below) and **magistrates** and **legal representatives** (revised on page 55).

Roles and powers of the police

The **role** of the police is to **keep the public safe**. For example:

- They prevent crime by providing education in schools and in the community.
- They deter crime through patrolling in the community.
- They investigate and collect evidence of crime.

Police have the following **powers**.

Stop and search	Arrest and enter premises	Detain and charge
• To stop people in public and ask them to explain their actions. • To stop and search people if they have a reasonable suspicion that a person is about to commit, or has committed a crime.	• To arrest anyone they believe has committed a crime, is engaged in committing a crime, or who is about to break the law. • To use reasonable force in arresting someone or stopping and searching them. • To enter premises without permission to arrest someone or to save a life or to prevent a crime.	• To detain someone for 24 hours without charge. • To charge someone for a crime if they have enough evidence, present the evidence to the Crown Prosecution Service, and attend court to give evidence in criminal trials.

Roles and powers of judges

The **role** of judges includes:

- being in charge of trials
- keeping order in court
- upholding and interpreting the law.

Judges have the following **powers**.

Applying the law	Sentencing and outcomes	Setting precedent
• To apply the law as made by Parliament (statutory law) and case law (common law) to all cases they hear. • In criminal trials, to advise juries on points of law to make sure of a fair trial.	• To decide what punishment those found guilty by jury in Crown Court trials should receive. Sentences vary according to the type, circumstances and seriousness of the offence. • To use sentencing guidelines from the sentencing council/Act of Parliament. If these are not in existence, then Court of Appeal judgements may be considered. • In civil trials, to decide the outcome.	• To set a precedent by their interpretation of existing law that is then followed by other judges in future trials.

Now try this

Identify **two** roles performed by a judge in a criminal court in England or Wales.   (2)

England and Wales justice system 2

The justice system in England and Wales involves the roles and powers of **police** and **judges** (revised on page 54) and **magistrates** and **legal representatives** (revised below).

Roles and powers of magistrates

The **role** of magistrates is mainly to **hear criminal cases** in a Magistrates' Court.

- They are usually volunteers from a local community.
- They are not lawyers but have training in the role.
- Legal advisers assist them with specialist knowledge.
- They are also known as justices of the peace (JPs).

Magistrates have the following **powers**.

Hearing cases	Arrest and sentencing	Transferring cases
• To deal with minor cases in criminal law, such as criminal damage. • Some may deal with civil cases in their community, where they might sit in the family or youth courts.	• To issue a search warrant or warrant for arrest. • To grant bail or keep the accused in custody. • To give a sentence of up to six months for one offence and a maximum of 12 months for two or more offences. • To give a fine of an unlimited amount.	• To transfer serious criminal cases, that begin in the Magistrates' Court but are beyond their powers, to the Crown Court.

Roles and powers of legal representatives

The main **role** of legal representatives such as **solicitors** and **barristers** is to be **experts in the law**.

- They help to make the legal system fair.
- They provide legal advice concerning the detail and complexities of law to non-specialist clients.

Legal representatives have the following **powers**.

Roles and powers	Solicitors	Barristers
• To act on behalf of an accused person to represent their defence in court in criminal cases. • To work for the Crown to prosecute someone accused of a crime. • In civil cases, to work for the claimant **or** who the claim has been brought against.	• To **prepare cases** for clients and sometimes to also appear in court.	• To **represent** their clients in higher courts, such as the Court of Appeal.

Now try this

Identify **two** roles performed by a magistrate in a Magistrates' Court in England and Wales.   (2)

Roles of citizens

The justice system in England and Wales involves citizens in the legal system, including roles and responsibilities as jurors, magistrates, special constables, or members of a tribunal hearing.

Roles and responsibilities of jurors

A juror is a person who sits on a jury in a trial at Crown Court, representing the community.

Selection	Service	Verdict
• Twelve jurors are required. Anyone aged between 18 and 70 (with some exceptions) can be selected at random. • Once selected, it is a civic duty to serve – a legal responsibility that cannot be turned down.	• Jury service usually lasts around two weeks but could be much longer. Employers must allow time off. Expenses are paid and compensation for loss of earnings if an employer does not pay you. • Jurors swear an oath to hear a case fairly and truly. They are responsible for listening to the evidence in the trials.	• Jurors meet after hearing the evidence to discuss their verdict. They must not communicate with others. Phones and other devices are removed. • They decide if evidence points to the defendant being guilty or not guilty, beyond reasonable doubt, giving the verdict in court.

Roles and responsibilities of members of tribunal hearings

Tribunals usually sit as a panel, including a legally qualified chairman and citizens with specific areas of expertise who are paid a fee and hear cases for at least 15 days a year.

Tribunals	Hearings	Outcomes
• Tribunals are like courts but are more informal. They are part of the civil justice system and can take evidence from claimants and respondents. • There are about 130 types of tribunal that deal with around one million cases every year.	• Tribunals hear disputes concerning employment, immigration and criminal injuries. They may be involved in decisions about benefits or provision of special educational help for school-aged children. • They hear evidence and decide the case themselves.	• Depending on the case, tribunals may have limited powers for fines, penalties, compensation and costs.

Magistrates and special constables

Magistrates are volunteers involved in the local community, rather than specialist judges with legal training. To revise their roles and responsibilities, see page 54.

Special constables are volunteers from all backgrounds who assist the police. When trained, they have the same responsibilities as the police (see page 53).

Benefits of involving citizens

There are **two** key areas of benefit when involving ordinary citizens ('lay' people who are not qualified experts) in the legal process.

- **Practical benefits** include cost efficiency and experience from all walks of life.
- **Theoretical benefits** include links with democracy, using juries to represent the community.

Now try this

Suggest **three** ways in which citizens can be involved in the justice system.   (3)

Law in practice

The justice system in England and Wales ensures that fundamental principles of the law are upheld in practice, such as the rights of citizens on arrest to **know the reason for arrest**, to **inform someone** of their arrest and to **see a solicitor**.

Right to know reason of arrest

The police have the responsibility to inform a person about the reason why they are being arrested so the justice process is fair.

- It would violate the person's human rights for the police to put them in a cell without telling them why.

- It links to the right to a fair trial and the rule of law (see page 49). A fair trial would not be possible if a person did not know why they had been arrested. They would not be able to defend themselves against any charges that were brought against them.

Right to inform of arrest

After a person has been arrested, they have a right to inform someone else about what has happened to them, for **three** main reasons.

1. To let someone know where they are.
2. For the police to contact an appropriate adult who must be present during questioning and searching if the person arrested is under 18, or is a vulnerable adult.
3. It is important to show that the citizen is not being subjected to unlawful treatment by the police.

Right to see a solicitor

After being arrested, a citizen has the right to consult with a legal representative for impartial advice that is free and independent of the police.

- Before starting questioning, the police must inform the arrested person that they have this right.

- This ensures that people are protected against unfair treatment by having access to legal advice.

- Most people will call a solicitor. If they do not have their own solicitor, a duty solicitor is available 24 hours a day at the police station, and is independent of the police.

- The police may also contact the Defence Solicitor Call Centre (DSCC).

If the arrested person is suspected of having committed a less serious offence, such as being drunk or disorderly, they may have a solicitor see them in person or be offered legal advice by phone.

Explaining rights

The custody officer at the police station must explain the citizen's rights. They also include the right to:

- medical help if feeling ill
- see the rules the police must follow
- see a written notice about their rights during their time in detention, such as regular breaks to use the toilet and access to food.

Now try this

Suggest **two** reasons why the police should respect the rights of the people they arrest. (2)

Criminal courts

Magistrates' Courts and **Crown Courts** are types of criminal court. There are key differences between how they operate and the types of cases they are used for.

Criminal cases start in the Magistrates' Court and most are completed there.

More serious cases are heard by the Crown Court for trial by judge and jury.

Cases heard by magistrates

Magistrates' Courts are used for less serious types of cases, known as **summary offences** such as minor motoring offences, criminal damage and minor assaults.

'Either way' offences

Some '**either way**' offences can be heard in a Magistrates' Court or a Crown Court and defendants have a right to ask for trial by a jury, such as burglary/theft and some drugs offences.

Cases heard in Crown Courts

Crown Courts are used for more serious types of cases, known as **indictable offences.** They are heard by the Crown Court as they require a trial by judge and jury, such as murder, rape and robbery.

Crown Court judges

High Court judges try very serious cases, such as murder and rape.

Circuit judges and **Recorders** try less serious cases such as theft, referred from the Magistrates' Court.

How Magistrates' Courts operate

In the Magistrates' Court:

- **three magistrates** hear each case, usually volunteers from all walks of life, with a range of experience. A district judge may hear more complex summary trials
- **a legal adviser** is on hand to provide guidance on points of law
- **magistrates pass sentences** of up to six months in prison and **set unlimited fines.**
- appeals from the Magistrates' Court are heard in the Crown Court.

How Crown Courts operate

In the Crown Court:

- **a judge** presides over cases and ensures they are fair – but the judge does not decide guilt
- **a jury** of 12 citizens, independent of the police and courts to ensure a fair trial, is selected at random, hears evidence, discusses the case and decides if the defendant is guilty or not.
- **the judge advises** the jury on the law and **sets the sentence** for a person the jury has found guilty.
- **appeals** from the Crown Court may be heard in the High Court and may go on to higher courts.

Now try this

Give an example of **one** type of case heard in a Magistrates' Court and **one** type of case heard in a Crown Court.

(2)

Civil courts

County Courts and High Courts are both types of civil courts with key differences in the way they are used. In civil law, parties are encouraged to cooperate and settle the case.

Most civil cases heard in the County Courts are less complex cases, or those involving smaller amounts of money. Appeals go to the High Court.

How County Courts are used

County Courts are used for civil cases such as:

* **disputes** about property, or breaches of contract between companies and individuals
* cases seeking **payment of debts**
* cases seeking to gain **compensation** for personal injury
* **small claims** of up to £10,000.

County Court process

* Cases can be dealt with via online written evidence without attending court.
* An out-of-court settlement may be reached.
* People can defend themselves, hire a solicitor or barrister to represent them or, with permission, allow a relative or advice worker to speak for them.
* Judgement is delivered after the judge has heard the evidence.
* Cases do not usually lead to punishment, but judges can award compensation or damages.
* Judges can issue an injunction – an order for one party not to do something, for example, to prevent them making noise in the early hours.

How High Courts are used

The High Court has **three** divisions that deal with civil cases.

① **The Queen's Bench Division** deals with **contractual issues**, such as breach of contract, and **civil wrongs**, such as those against the person, including defamation and libel. It also deals with wrongs against **property**, such as trespass, and wrongs against **people or property**, such as negligence or nuisance.

② **The Family Division** deals with appeals from family law courts. It also deals with orders giving custody of under 18s to the court, where care is carried out by an individual or by a local authority.

③ **The Chancery Division** deals with resolution of disputes involving matters such as company law, land law, patents and mortgages. It also deals with insolvency and professional negligence.

The High Court hears civil cases that are too complex for County Courts, or where large sums of money are involved. Cases are usually heard by a single judge. **Circuit judges** and **Recorders** may also hear cases. Appeals go to the Court of Appeal.

Now try this

Name **one** type of case the County Court deals with.   (1)

Tribunals

The justice system includes the use of tribunals and other means of civil dispute resolution, such as mediation, to settle disputes.

How tribunals are used

There are around 130 types of tribunal. Most cases are held in public, involving disputes affecting daily life such as:

- employment
- immigration
- lands
- criminal injury
- mental health
- pensions.

Tribunal Chair

Tribunals are similar to courts. They are legally binding but less formal, less expensive and a faster way to resolve disputes. The system is divided between First-tier Tribunal, and Upper Tribunal, which reviews and decides appeals from First-tier Tribunal, and can call on the services of judges.

The process in tribunals

Here are **three** key points about tribunals.

1. Cases are heard by a panel of three members. The chair person has legal training. The others are citizens with expertise in the issues.

2. Claimants and respondents give evidence. Individuals may put their own case without a solicitor or lawyer and are expertly guided through the process.

3. When all evidence is heard, a decision is given that day, or later in writing. The tribunal has powers to set fines, or award compensation and costs.

Other civil dispute resolution

Other means of settling civil disputes may be cheaper than involving the legal system. For example, alternative dispute resolution (ADR) allows parties to settle disputes with the mediation of a third party.

ADR is independent, impartial and free of charge. It is only interested in finding a solution.

Mediation

Other means of civil dispute resolution include negotiation, conciliation and arbitration. These may be assisted in **two** ways.

1 Mediation

A trained, impartial third party works with disputing parties to help reach agreement. It can be cheaper and quicker than court. For example, cases can be mediated by phone, sometimes within an hour.

2 Ombudsmen

Ombudsmen are appointed to look into complaints about companies and organisations without going to court, for areas such as energy and financial services. They investigate cases of injustice and make recommendations to put things right.

Now try this

Suggest **two** reasons why mediation as a method of settling disputes could be better than going to court.

(2)

Youth justice

The justice system for young people under 18 differs from the system that deals with adults. Provisions are made in their contact with police and the court system which differs from other courts.

Youth justice and the police

When young people are arrested, they have a right when being searched, questioned and interviewed to be accompanied by an appropriate responsible adult. This can be a parent, guardian or carer. If the offender admits guilt and the offence is not serious enough for court, a **caution** is given, and the young person's needs are assessed by a **Youth Offending Team (YOT)** in relation to rehabilitation and education.

Offenders aged under 10

Offenders under 10 are given a local child curfew to be at home between 9pm and 6am unless they are with an adult. They are referred to Youth Offending Teams (YOTs) for support and rehabilitation.

Youth courts

Most cases involving defendants aged 10 to 17 are heard in a **youth court**, which is a type of Magistrates' Court.

- Cases such as **theft, burglary, anti-social behaviour** and **drugs offences** are dealt with.
- Three magistrates **or** a judge hears the case, with **no** jury.
- They take account of age, seriousness of offence, previous record, guilty plea, and mitigating circumstances.

Sentencing

A parent or guardian must be with the young person if they are under 16, or aged 16–17 and given a court order.

- If convicted, a range of sentences can be given, including **fines, community sentences** and **detention and training orders** in secure centres for young people.
- Prison is **not** used, as this may encourage re-offending (see page 61).
- A **conditional** or **absolute discharge** may be given, if arrest and the court experience is considered punishment enough.

Youth courts are **less formal** than adult courts. Defendants are called by their first name and, to protect their identity, the public are usually not allowed to watch. For serious crimes such as murder or rape, the case starts in the youth court and is then passed to the Crown Court where extended and life sentences may be given.

Now try this

Explain **one** way that youth courts differ from other courts.   (2)

Youth sentencing

The **Crime and Disorder Act 1998** reformed the system to help young offenders under 18, often from troubled backgrounds, not to reoffend. It changed from retributive justice (punishment such as prison, that protects the public and takes revenge on offenders) to:

- **rehabilitation**, for example, community sentencing, education, and training to reform offenders.

- **restorative justice** such as community sentencing and fines, so offenders give back to society.

Community sentences

There are **three** main community sentences for young people, which are different from those for adults. A young person who breaks the rules could end up back in court.

1. **Referral orders**: the young person agrees to a programme of work to address behaviour with a panel of people from the local community and youth justice workers.

2. **Reparation orders**: the young person makes up for the harm caused, by repairing damage to the victim's property, for example.

3. **Youth rehabilitation orders**: the court decides what the offender must do for up to three years, to help them rehabilitate and become law-abiding. For example, receiving drug treatment, or being under curfew.

Community sentences aim to prevent reoffending through intensive unpaid work that punishes the offender, alongside education and rehabilitation through treatment or training programmes.

Detention and training orders

A detention and training order can be given to offenders aged 12–17, and may last between four months and two years. The first half is served in custody in a secure centre for young people (not an adult prison), and the rest in the community.

Restorative justice

Restorative justice is part of a community sentence. It aims to repair the harm done by an offenders' actions and restore balance. It may involve listening to their victim about the impact of their crime, and apologising in a letter or in person.

Youth Offending Teams (YOTs)

YOTs are independent of the police and courts. They are part of the local council.

- They work with police, health and education teams, probation officers, charities, and the community to rehabilitate offenders.

- They help safeguard welfare and prevent reoffending through dealing with the young person's problems. This may involve drug or alcohol treatment, or courses in anger management and decision-making.

- They may attend court with the young person and supervise community service.

Now try this

Explain **one** reason why restorative justice is often used with young offenders. (2)

Crime rates

When considering whether crime is increasing in society, it is important to consider the factors affecting crime rates. These include issues around the recording of crime and reasons for reoffending.

Key crimes

Key crime types in society include violence, homicide (murder and manslaughter), firearms offences, robbery and theft (including mugging), cybercrimes (including identity theft and fraud), fraud, sexual offences, public order offences and criminal damage.

Factors affecting crime rates

Factors affecting crime rates in society include rises in unemployment, poverty, social and family breakdown and abuse, misuse of drugs and alcohol, new kinds of crimes, such as cyber crimes, changing morals and freedoms, age of the population, police policies for reporting and recording crime, rate of reoffending.

Reporting and recording of crime

Many factors affect crime statistics. Here are **three** examples:

1. **Level of accuracy.** The way the police record crimes may affect the number of crimes reported. The Home Office sets rules on what counts as crime which the police follow, to improve accuracy.

2. **More people reporting crimes** results in an increase in crime rates, rather than more crimes actually taking place.

3. **Fewer people reporting crimes** means more crimes may take place than are reported.

Reasons for not reporting crimes

Reasons for not reporting crimes include:

- not detecting the crime (for example, online financial fraud)
- being embarrassed about being a crime victim and not wanting others to know
- being afraid the criminal will take revenge or carry out the offence on the victim again
- not wanting to get the offender into trouble
- a lack of trust and confidence in the police or the justice system to deal with the offender
- fear they will be treated as a suspect rather than a victim
- not wanting the additional stress and inconvenience of getting involved in an investigation.

Crime rates in society

There can be a conflict between the **perception** and **reality** of crime rates.

- **Perception of an increase in crime rates** can be influenced by media.
- **Statistics show overall crime rates falling** for two decades.

Reasons for reoffending

Crime rates are affected by the number of people who reoffend. Here are some reasons.

- They may have no home and no job. Prison provides shelter, food and healthcare.
- They may have become 'institutionalised' by prison, unable to survive outside the system.
- They may need to fund a drug addiction.
- They may learn 'tricks of the trade' from offenders in prison, and carry out more crime

Now try this

Explain **two** reasons why people may not report crimes. (4)

Reducing crime

Strategies to reduce crime in society include **prevention**, **protection** and **punishment**.

Prevention

Prevention aims to stop crime happening by **removing the causes for offences**.

Method	Why it could be effective
Increasing community policing, through the use of high visibility patrols, and police visits to schools to talk to young people	✓ Prevents crime by relationship-building with police and learning to avoid crime.
Providing high quality education	✓ Improves opportunities, so crime is less attractive.
Providing counselling for drug and alcohol problems	✓ Helps people to stop abusing drugs or alcohol and keep away from crime, as funding addiction often leads to crime.
Providing positive opportunities for young people, such as youth clubs	✓ Involves young people in activities so they do not turn to crime out of boredom.

Protection

Protection aims to reduce crime through **measures to protect society**.

Method	Why it could be effective
Security measures, such as CCTV, alarms, locking and alerting devices	✓ Protects people and property by putting off potential criminals if they know they may be caught.
Neighbourhood Watch schemes	✓ Crimes are less likely if observers notice activity.
Improving the community, for example, increased street lighting, keeping a neighbourhood clean and orderly	✓ Crimes are less likely if improved conditions show up criminal behaviour. Suspicious activities are more out of place in communities that are cared for.

Punishment

Punishment aims to reduce crime by **deterring** people who fear the consequences of their actions.

- It shows that criminal actions are unacceptable.
- It ranges in strength according to the crime.
- Prison is the most severe punishment in the UK.
- The UK aims to rehabilitate offenders to reduce crime.
- Punishment used for first-time offenders often includes conditional discharge, community service or fines.
- Punishments include prison, conditional discharge, fines, electronic tagging, and community payback (unpaid community work).

Prison is a powerful punishment used for serious crime where loss of freedom can deter (discourage) potential offenders. Facilities include the state-run system and a number of privately managed prisons.

Now try this

Explain how **one** way of preventing crime could be effective.

(2)

Sentence and punishment

Different types of sentence and punishment are determined for different offences.

Types of sentence and how they are determined

Judges and magistrates follow Sentencing Council guidelines when deciding what type of sentence is justified. They weigh up the aggravating and mitigating factors, including the seriousness of the crime, the level of harm to the victim, the offender's age, criminal record, circumstances, level of blame and whether they have pleaded guilty.

Type of sentence	How the sentence is determined
Imprisonment • The offender is 'locked up' – detained in prison. • The aim is to protect the public from danger and to exercise retribution through loss of freedom. • A **determinate** sentence means the offender spends half the time in prison and the rest out on licence, but they can be returned to prison if they reoffend. • An **indeterminate** sentence has no fixed length. • A **minimum** term may be given with no release until the offender is proven not to be a threat.	• Used for the most serious offences such as murder, rape, or for repeat offenders.
Fines • The offender is ordered to pay a sum of money. • The aim is to hurt the offender financially and deter future similar crimes.	• Used for less serious, non-violent offences, such as theft or minor driving offences.
Community payback • The offender carries out up to 300 hours of unpaid work, such as gardening, litter-picking or painting. • The aim is to reform offenders by showing that actions have consequences and reinforcing positive action.	• Often used with first-time offenders for offences such as vandalism, petty theft, non-grievous assault, shoplifting.
Electronic tagging • The offender wears an electronic device to monitor location and curfew times. • The aim is to reduce the opportunity for future offences and change the offender's behaviour.	• May be used as part of a prisoner's terms of licence when they are released from prison.
Sentences involving restorative justice • The offender meets the victim to hear the impact of the crime and to apologise. • The aim is for the offender to realise how their actions affect people and to change their behaviour.	• Often used for young offenders aged 10–17 as part of a referral order, and first-time youth offenders who plead guilty.

Now try this

Give **two** types of sentence, other than prison, used to deal with crime in the UK. (2)

The purpose of punishment

There are debates about the purpose and impact of different types of punishment, including prison, community payback and restorative justice.

Types of punishment

Different types of punishment are intended to protect the public, and act as:

- **deterrence** – putting people off committing crime
- **rehabilitation** – reforming the criminal so they stop offending
- **retribution** – getting revenge on the criminal
- **restitution** – putting things right for the victim, and society.

Debates on the purpose and impact of punishment

Points for the punishment	Points against the punishment
Deterrence (any punishment)	
• Fear of punishment discourages potential offenders. • Individual deterrence is aimed at putting a specific offender off committing crimes. • General deterrence is aimed at putting the whole population off committing crimes, as the penalties are strong and clear.	• Prisoner numbers keep going up, which suggests deterrence does not work and has little impact. In 2018, the UK had a prison population of 80,000, which is 146 per 100,000 people.
Rehabilitation (e.g. community payback)	
• Reforming offenders is increasingly encouraged to help them become law-abiding citizens. • The rehabilitation chosen takes into account and addresses the circumstances of the offence.	• If many offenders reoffend it suggests that the impact of rehabilitation is limited.
Retribution / retributive justice (e.g. prison)	
• Offenders deserve to be punished for breaking the rules of society. • Retribution is the only way they will learn their behaviour is unacceptable and allow the victims or their families to feel that justice has been done.	• Seeking revenge is counter-productive and does little to change behaviour. • Retribution can have the opposite effect by making offenders resentful and more likely to commit more crimes.
Restitution / restorative justice (e.g. community payback, fines)	
• It is only fair that offenders give something back, as they have taken something from society.	• Many people feel these are not real punishments and that the offender has got away with their crime, so justice is not seen to be done. Restorative justice may be seen as an easy option when compared with prison.

Now try this

Using an example, explain what is meant by restorative justice. (2)

This type of question tests both your knowledge and understanding of a term.

Short answer questions

In **Paper 1, Section C,** questions are focused on **Theme C: Law and justice.**

> ### Paper 1 Section C short answer questions
>
> Short answer questions require you to demonstrate your knowledge and understanding of citizenship concepts, terms and issues. Here are command words you might see:
>
> - **which, give, identify, name:** you need to give a point or example without further development.
> - **explain:** you need to make a point and then develop it to show your understanding.
> - **suggest:** you need to show your understanding when reasons are less clear cut.

Worked example

Explain the meaning of 'presumption of innocence'. **(2)**

It means that every defendant is assumed to be innocent until proven guilty in court. It is a fundamental principle of English law, and the prosecution has to prove that a person is guilty.

'Explain' questions require you to make a point and then develop it.

The definition shows knowledge of meaning and the development shows understanding of the principle.

Suggest **three** ways in which laws can regulate behaviour. **(3)**

1 Defining unacceptable behaviour.

2 Punishing unacceptable behaviour.

3 Treating everybody the same.

'Suggest' questions test your understanding.

You do not need to develop or explain the simple points you make.

Which of these is true of youth courts in England and Wales? **(1)**

☐ **A** They deal with young offenders aged 8–18.

☐ **B** They treat young offenders like adults.

☐ **C** They have a jury for really serious offences.

☒ **D** They can give 9-year-olds a Local Child Curfew.

Read all the answers carefully. Eliminate answers that are incorrect and choose the correct answer.

Give **two** reasons why Scotland has different laws to England and Wales. **(2)**

1 Scotland had its own legal system when it joined the UK.

2 Today Scotland has its own parliament which has the power to make its own laws.

'Give' questions test your knowledge. You do not need to give a developed answer. Provide enough information to make your answer clear.

Identify **one** role of a magistrate. **(1)**

Deciding on the guilt of a defendant.

Now try this

Using an example, explain what is meant by retributive justice. **(2)**

This type of question tests both your knowledge, and understanding of a term.

Source C questions 1

In **Paper 1, Section C,** you will need to apply your knowledge and understanding of citizenship concepts, terms and issues to contexts and actions as you respond to a source.

Paper 1 Section C Source C questions

One question in **Section C: Law and justice** is based on Source C. You will need to read the source and then answer a question about it. Here are command words you might see:

- **explain:** you need to provide a reasoned explanation that shows your understanding through justifying or giving examples of the points you have identified, applied to a source.

- **compare:** you need to compare two or more issues, opinions or situations.

Source C

Study Source C and then answer the question on the next page.

> Read the source carefully. It relates to the question on page 69, which is about explaining why youth courts are different from other courts.

Source C: The youth justice system in England and Wales

The Crime and Disorder Act 1998 reformed the youth justice system. It aimed to discourage young people from offending or reoffending, and <u>created multi-agency Young Offending Teams (YOTs) from professional agencies</u> to work with young people. These agencies were <u>legally obliged to work</u> together and exchange information to develop more <u>effective ways of dealing with juvenile offenders.</u>

Young people charged with an offence appear in <u>special youth courts</u> presided over by magistrates. These are <u>less formal and threatening</u> than adult courts and provide <u>swift justice</u>. They are meant to show young people the consequences of antisocial behaviour. Magistrates deal with young offenders in <u>different ways</u> but refer the more serious offences to a Crown Court for sentencing. Fewer than 4% of juvenile cases are referred to a Crown Court.

From March 2017 to March 2018 almost 1,000 young people were sentenced in Crown Courts. Around 500 received custodial sentences. By contrast, nearly <u>22,000 young offenders were sentenced in youth courts, but only 5% received custodial sentences</u>. Magistrates prefer to give sentences which <u>will rehabilitate wrongdoers</u> and <u>discourage reoffending</u>.

> Underlining key points can help focus your answer. Here, for example, consider points relating to:
>
> - reforms in the youth justice system which affected youth courts
> - how the system is designed to be effective for young offenders
> - referring to the Crown Court serious offences such as murder and rape
> - avoiding custodial (prison) sentences
> - sentences available to youth courts such as community service, fines, youth rehabilitation orders and their purposes
> - concern for rehabilitation rather than retribution.

Now try this

The source refers to Youth Offending Teams. Give **two** roles of these teams. **(2)**

Source C questions 2

This response to an **explain** question relates to the source on page 68. It shows the qualities your answer to an 'explain' question should demonstrate:

- detailed knowledge about the concepts, terms and issues relevant to the question
- good understanding of how they apply by effective and sustained comment about the source context.

Worked example

Source C shows how the youth justice system in England and Wales was set up and how youth courts work.

Explain, with reference to Source C, why youth courts are different from adult courts. **(6)**

When the youth justice system was reformed in 1998, it changed focus from a retributive justice system to a rehabilitation and restorative system. Youth courts were given the responsibility of safeguarding young offenders' welfare, to prevent reoffending and to reduce custodial sentences. Imprisonment was seen as a major cause of reoffending because it meant young offenders would mix with and learn from hardened criminals.

The youth courts and proceedings are less formal than adult courts, so less threatening in terms of dress and layout. There is no jury and no public access, so the privacy of young offenders is protected. The press is allowed to report proceedings but not to give details of their names, schools or families. The defendant is called by their first name and supported by an adult. A responsible adult is required for all accused under the age of 16. The result is a reduction in offenders appearing in youth courts, with increased use of police caution for minor offences.

The YOTs prepare and present multi-agency reports for the court and supervise rehabilitation programmes. The youth courts deal with less serious offences such as theft, antisocial behaviour and drug offences. Serious offences (rape, murder) are referred to Crown Courts. Youth courts use a range of options to avoid custodial sentences such as community service and fines. The court may also give an absolute or conditional discharge.

Magistrates take account of the age, the seriousness of offence, any previous record, a guilty plea, and mitigating circumstances. Youth courts deal with young people before they are long-time offenders and aim to set up rehabilitation plans to reduce reoffending.

This question relates to Source C (page 68) and includes own knowledge.

Read the question carefully. You are only asked about why youth courts are **different** from adult courts.

This shows good understanding of key terms. Information in the source is put to good use.

This uses information in the source **along with** explanation and own knowledge, with sustained comment.

Now try this

Explain **two** reasons why we have youth courts. **(4)**

Practice short answer questions

Practise for **Paper 1, Section C**, with these exam-style short answer questions. Example answers are provided (page 132 forward).

Guided

Explain **one** way in which criminal courts differ from civil courts. **(2)**

....

....

....

> Contrast the work of the two types of court.

Suggest **one** sentence that magistrates might impose on a first-time offender. **(1)**

....

> The answer does not need to be developed.

The term 'common law' refers to laws which are: **(1)**

- ☐ **A** based on statutes passed by parliament
- ☐ **B** interpretations of the law made by judges when giving verdicts
- ☐ **C** made by the Scottish parliament
- ☐ **D** imposed by the EU on member states.

> Read the options carefully then select the correct choice.

Give **one** right that is legal for the first time at the age of 16. **(1)**

....

> Don't suggest what can be done before 16.

Identify the court a person might appear in if prosecuted for speeding. **(1)**

....

> No development is needed.

Explain **two** different ways in which laws can be made in the UK. **(4)**

1 ....

....

....

2 ....

....

....

> It is not enough only to state different sources of law. Explain the different ways in more detail.

Had a look ☐   Nearly there ☐   Nailed it! ☐

Practice Source C questions

Practise for **Paper 1, Section C**, with this exam-style source question. Apply **your** knowledge and understanding of citizenship concepts, terms and issues in the context of the source. Example answers are provided at the end of this book.

Guided

Study Source C and then answer the question below.

> **Source C: Prison in the United States**
>
> The main punishment in the USA is imprisonment in either a state or federal prison. In 2016, 90% of prisoners were in state or federal facilities. Since 1980, with a rapidly increasing prison population, some prisons have been privatised, but a government report in 2016 condemned them as 'less safe, less secure, and more punitive' than federal prisons. Some states imprison debtors and solitary confinement is widely used. Many prisoners are non-violent, poor, mentally ill or drug addicts.
>
> Prison rates in the USA in 1980 were comparable with other developed countries. Since then, the prison population has increased dramatically because of the 'war on drugs' and President Reagan's 'tough on crime' policy. Compulsory sentencing imposes minimum sentences. Judges have lost their discretionary sentencing power and cannot take account of extenuating circumstances. 'Three strikes and you're out' laws mean violent offenders with two previous sentences may automatically receive a life sentence.
>
> In 2016, the USA had 655 prisoners for every 100,000 adults. Canada had 114, the UK 139, and Australia 172. The Netherlands had 61 and Japan only 41. One-fifth of the world's 10.3 million prisoners are in the USA.

Source C is about imprisonment in the USA. Using Source C and your own knowledge compare approaches to imprisonment in the UK and America. **(6)**

• Read the source and question carefully. Underline relevant information in the source to help you focus your answer.

• You do not need to know more about imprisonment in the USA than is in the source.

Show your knowledge and understanding of prison in the UK in comparison to the source information. Do not simply write out or summarise what the source says.

Contrast the USA with the UK. You could consider the state-run prison system, privately run prisons, that solitary confinement is not widely used in the UK, and the use of different sentencing options. Similarities might include criticism of some conditions, and some political parties advocating a 'tough on crime' approach.

Remember that there are different legal systems in England, Northern Ireland and Scotland. You could include these in your comparisons.

Compare the tight control on sentencing in the USA with the guidance given to judges in the UK and their ability to vary sentences to take account of individual circumstances and previous records.

Compare numbers in prison and considerations of the purposes and impact of imprisonment and other kinds of punishment in the UK.

Use a separate piece of paper to answer this question.

Source D questions 1

In **Paper 1, Section D**, questions are focused on **citizenship issues and debates**. The extended-response questions relate to two or more of Themes A to C of your course.

Paper 1 Section D Source D questions

One question in **Section D: Citizenship issues and debates** is based on Source D. The source may be divided into parts and is about different viewpoints.

The question is divided into parts:

- short answer questions (see page 73)
- a long answer question that requires extended writing (see page 74).

Source D

Source D: Should 16-year-olds be given the vote? Emily Thornberry says YES

In 1918, the basic right to vote was extended to some women. How long do we have to wait until the vote is extended to everyone over 16? <u>We led the way in recognising that 18-year-olds were adults by giving them the vote in 1969. It will be the same again.</u> <u>There is no logical explanation for the different rights that we give to 16-year-olds.</u> Free from parental control, they can leave home, start a family, get married, start work, pay taxes and join the forces. Is there a logical reason to deny them the right to vote on <u>issues that will affect them once old enough to make other decisions?</u>

Last year, over 2,000 16 and 17-year-olds received a carer's allowance for looking after disabled relatives. <u>Is it fair and logical to give them that responsibility but deny them a vote?</u>

There is no logical objection to votes at 16. That is why the <u>Welsh and Scottish Governments support it, as do every political party in the House</u> except the Conservatives and the Democratic Unionists. When <u>change is right it cannot be resisted forever.</u> This is a change whose time has come.

Source D gives different viewpoints on an issue. Start by reading the 'yes' viewpoint here.

Underlining key points can help focus your answer. Here, for example, consider points relating to:

- the UK as a leader in electoral reform
- the UK as illogical in what it allows those aged 16 to do - how far is this convincing?
- those aged 16 being affected by issues made by those elected – a main argument for extending the vote
- evidence that supports the argument, such as the number of carers denied a vote
- the viewpoints of regional assemblies
- a conclusion suggesting the Conservatives and DUP are reactionary and resisting inevitable change.

Now read the 'no' viewpoint on page 73.

Source D questions 2

Source D starts on page 72 and continues below.

Source D

Source D: Should 16-year-olds be given the vote? David Lidington says NO

Eighteen <u>is recognised as the age at which one becomes an adult</u> and when full citizenship rights are attained. Only a handful of countries have a nationwide voting age below 18. The Conservative government believes that 18 should continue to be the age at which people become eligible to vote.

The <u>last Labour government raised the legal age</u> for buying cigarettes, selling knives, buying fireworks and using sunbeds to 18 because only then could people <u>be expected to have sufficient maturity and responsibility</u>. It is perfectly reasonable to say that, from 18 we should trust young people to exercise those rights and responsibilities in full.

School councils get young people <u>used to the idea of exercising democratic responsibility</u>. That is excellent <u>training for the full adult responsibilities they will inherit at 18.</u>

Many youth organisations work hard to get young people used to the idea that they should take an interest in current affairs, and when they reach the relevant age, exercise their full political rights and responsibilities. <u>A national voting age at 18, is followed by 26 out of the 27 other members of the EU</u> and by the United States, Canada, New Zealand and Australia. <u>We should treat this subject seriously.</u>

When you have also read the 'no' viewpoint here about votes at 16, you will be able to analyse arguments for and against the issue. When you give your own opinion, you must be prepared to explain and justify it, and say why you disagree with the other opinion.

The argument is that 18 is the generally accepted age for full citizenship. Consider whether this is a good argument for opposing change.

The argument is that Labour is inconsistent. Members want to lower the voting age but other decisions showed they thought under 18s were not mature enough. Consider how fair it is to compare rules about safety with voting.

David Lidington argues that people need to learn to vote sensibly before they have full responsibility, and talks about possible ways of learning.

The conclusion repeats the opening claim and gives evidence to support it. Consider how far the argument is convincing.

The conclusion implies that Labour is not treating the issue of voting at 16 seriously, but that the Conservative government is.

Now try this

From reading the source, give **two** reasons why Emily Thornberry thought 16-year-olds should have the vote and two reasons why David Lidington thought 16-year-olds should not have the vote.

Short answer questions

In **Paper 1, Section D**, questions are focused on **citizenship issues and debates**.

Paper 1 Section D Source D short answer questions

Some questions will require short answers, including multiple choice questions. The questions will assess your understanding and analysis of the source.

Worked example

Study Source D about giving the vote to 16-year-olds. Then answer the questions that follow.

Which of the following does Emily Thornberry believe? **(1)**

- ☐ **A** Only 16-year-olds who have cared for parents should be given the vote.
- ☐ **B** Only 16-year-olds who have shown responsibility should be given the vote.
- ☐ **C** All 16-year-olds should have the vote for things that affect them.
- ☒ **D** All 16-year-olds should have the vote, according to the governments of Scotland and Wales.

Which of the following is a reason David Lidington gives for reducing the voting age? **(1)**

- ☐ **A** Labour was wrong when it raised the age for buying cigarettes and fireworks to 18.
- ☐ **B** Most 16-year-olds are content to exercise their vote in school council elections.
- ☒ **C** In most European and English-speaking states, the voting age remains at 18.
- ☐ **D** A handful of countries have a voting age below 18 and this is reasonable.

Analyse Source D and identify **two** views on which both writers agree. **(2)**

1 Voting is about having full citizenship rights.

2 The Conservative Party is opposed to giving 16-year-olds the vote.

These two multiple-choice questions assess your understanding of Source D on pages 71–72. You will need this understanding when answering the long answer question which carries higher marks.

You should eliminate some of the answers quite easily to narrow the answers you need to choose from. For example, A and B can be eliminated because they use the word 'only' and the passage is about votes for **all** 16-year-olds. C implies that the vote should be given for some things but not for everything.

A can be eliminated, for example, because this point is meant to illustrate that Labour thought younger people were not ready for responsibility.

B can be eliminated because, although he said school councils offered training in voting, he did not suggest 16-year-olds were content with this.

D can be eliminated because it is not stated that this is reasonable.

'Analyse' questions require you to examine the source and assess your understanding and analysis of it. Here, you have to identify views in both parts of the source to comment on similarities in viewpoints.

Now try this

Analyse Source D to identify **one** further issue about which the two writers agree.

 It will help your answer to the long question if you can identify areas of agreement as well as disagreement in the viewpoints.

Long answer question

One part of the question on Source D will require you to analyse and evaluate different viewpoints as you explain which writer you agree with more.

Paper 1 Section D Source D long answer question

This question requires extended writing that shows the following qualities:

- A convincing and sustained analysis of the different views expressed in the source.
- Reasoned, coherent arguments that show breadth and depth in your evaluation.
- Judgements about which writer you agree with more, which you substantiate with reasons.

Worked example

Which writer do you agree with more? Explain your answer, referring to the arguments made in both parts of the source.   **(12 marks)**

Lidington argues against change, preferring to keep things as they are, with 18 as the traditional age of adulthood, but Thornberry argues in favour of change. Thornberry says the UK has led most of the world in expanding and extending the electorate, but Lidington is content to carry on doing what other countries do.

Thornberry argues that many 16-year-olds already show responsibility (such as caring for relatives) and are legally allowed to do things that encourage an independent life. Lidington stresses their immaturity and the need to be trained and prepared to exercise responsibility later on. Thornberry recognises that 16-year-olds are concerned about real issues, and should be able to influence things that affect them. Thornberry says it is illogical to allow some things at 16 but not others. Lidington claims Labour raised some age limits because of a lack of maturity in those under 18. This argument is weak because the changes were about health and safety, not about decision-making. These are different things. Thornberry argues that voting at 16 is allowed in some parts of the UK for some elections and is supported by most parties. Lidington ignores this and makes no reference to alternative practices or the views of other parties.

Both writers criticise, directly or by implication, the policies of their opponents. Just because votes at 18 is what we are used to doesn't mean that it is right. Thornberry makes a good case for making a change. I think she presents the stronger and more consistent argument because she recognises the qualities of those aged 16, but Lidington seems happy to leave things as they are, although he does have a good point about Labour being inconsistent.

This question relates to Source D (see pages 71–72). Make sure you base your answer on the content of **both** parts of the source.

Both are selective in what they say and ignore what is inconvenient.

Identify the arguments presented by **each** of the writers, so your answer is not only about one viewpoint and not only your own opinion. This shows contrasting attitudes to maturity in young people, supported by reference to both parts of the source.

You don't have to agree with one viewpoint and reject the other. Evaluate both viewpoints and consider the evidence. Link and develop your points in a sustained way to reach a justified conclusion.

Now try this

Write a conclusion that agrees more with Lidington's viewpoint. Give reasons for supporting it.

Linked theme questions 1

One question in Section D will **state a point of view** related to citizenship issues and debates, and ask you **how far you agree** with it. You will be given **two linked areas of content** from Themes A–C that you are asked to consider in your answer.

Paper 1 Section D linked theme question

The question requires extended writing that shows the following qualities:

- A convincing and sustained analysis of relevant viewpoints on both sides of the argument.
- Reasoned, coherent arguments, showing good breadth and depth in your evaluation.
- An overall judgement that is well substantiated by the evidence provided.

An example starts below and continues on page 76.

Worked example

'Local councils can no longer rely on the funds they receive from central government and should limit themselves to providing the most basic and essential services.'

How far do you agree with this view?

Give reasons for your opinion, showing that you have considered different views on the topic.

In your answer you could consider:
- councils and the services they provide
- taxation and government spending.

(15)

When asked 'how far...', make sure your opinion is in context with reasons for holding it. Give a conclusion.

Local councils are democratically elected by their community as the government of their area and to provide services for electors. They have certain statutory duties set by Parliament but can also provide other services as each council chooses. It can be argued that electors vote for those councillors who they think will provide the services they want. All services cost money and the financial resources of councils are finite.

Be familiar with key terminology and concepts of the course (here, see Theme A and Theme B).

Council funding comes from government grants, council tax, business rates and charges for sales and services. The main contributor is the government. This means the government is in a strong position to influence local government spending. A basic economic principle is that spending should be within the resources available.

This shows knowledge of councils and develops into an opinion and evaluation.

One view put forward by the current government is that many councils are wasteful, inefficient and spend on projects that are not essential. Following the economic crisis of 2008, David Cameron's coalition government introduced a policy of austerity, and introduced severe cuts on government grants to councils. This forced councils to review spending plans, and focus on what was essential by making efficiency savings and cutting inessentials. The government has argued that councils must live within their means.

This shows knowledge of funding and the important role of central government.

This presents one view in support of the statement, giving reasons and justifying restrictions. It explains the points made and supports them with examples and evaluation.

Linked theme questions 2

The example **linked theme** question starts on page 75 and continues below.

Worked example

Some might argue that since most of a council's income comes from the government, the government is entitled to have a say about spending plans. The government doesn't have money of its own. It redistributes money taken from taxpayers. Austerity has hit taxpayers hard, and many have suffered from rising costs and no simultaneous rise in income. Is it fair that tax paid by taxpayers in areas where the council is careful should be used by the government to give money to extravagant councils?

A different view is that councils are elected democratically to obey their voters and not the government. Each council knows what its area needs and should be allowed to spend money on the services that are needed. If the government won't give the money, councils should be allowed to borrow or increase council tax. If the electors don't like this, they will vote them out of office.

A third view is that different areas of the country have different social and economic structures. Some areas are affluent but other areas are deprived and need more spent on essentials. Those that would most benefit from a wider range of services are those least able to afford them. Wealthier areas are less likely to need them, and will probably have money to spend on other things. Government grants should be distributed in a way that takes account of different needs.

We should remember that the purpose of local councils is to look after and provide for the needs of their community. Local people are better placed to decide what those needs are. The government should try to reduce waste and inefficiency, but it shouldn't harm local communities. Local authorities should be given sufficient resources to provide the services their constituents need. If the public don't agree with the council's priorities, they can always vote them out of office. If the government has to save money, it could cut some 'vanity projects' like HS2, aircraft carriers, Trident and overseas aid, and give that money to local authorities for services that people need.

This develops and expands the answer, showing analysis of the viewpoint with sustained comment and going on to address the second bullet point in the question.

You must consider a different point of view, continuing to show your analysis and evaluation skills. This addresses the first bullet in the question.

This further point of view shows a balanced approach, recognising different needs.

This recognises that both sides can present a strong case but comes to a clear conclusion that is justified on the basis of the democratic structure and the accountability of councillors to their constituents.

Now try this

Write a paragraph that comes to a different conclusion than the one given above.

Practice Source D questions 1

Practise for **Paper 1, Section D: Citizenship issues and debates**, with these exam style questions. Start by reading Source D below, then answer the questions on page 78.

Guided

Source D: Should taxes be reduced?

Owen Jones says NO

The journalist Owen Jones said the media criticised Labour's tax plans for being too extreme, but he thought they were not radical enough to meet Britain's economic needs. He said that Labour's proposed top rate of tax was lower than in the post-war period when, in spite of high taxes, the country prospered and living standards improved. Today, some countries with higher tax rates have stronger economies than the UK.

Jones argued that income tax should be cut for the poorest, but raised for the wealthiest 20%, with a top tax rate of 60%. He wanted Corporation Tax to be raised to 26%, still lower than any of the world's leading economies. He liked Scottish Labour's ideas for new property and land taxes, and a wealth tax on the richest 10%.

He suggested that Labour's plans were less radical than public opinion. A recent poll showed half the population wanted millionaires to pay a top rate of 75%. Another poll showed half of respondents wanted a top rate of 60% on earnings over £120,000 per year, and a third favoured taxing incomes over £300,000 at 80%. He argued that Britain needed a more radical approach.

Fraser Nelson says YES

Journalist Fraser Nelson argued that the Bank of England's policy of low interest rates and increased borrowing was not the solution for the UK's economic problems. He claimed that low interest rates are a subsidy for the wealthy at the expense of the poor. As a policy, it encourages inflation which increases prices and affects the poorest most heavily. The wealthy have grown richer faster than ever, but young people are priced out of home ownership.

He denied that all will share in economic recovery. He thought young people see no point saving or working hard because of the effect of low interest rates. The Prime Minister knows they are the hardest hit by austerity and has protected them with reduced taxes. Recognising that British business must be able to compete globally, she will cut Corporation Tax to 15%.

Nelson argued that tax cuts for the low paid will stimulate the economy by encouraging them to work and not rely on welfare. The policy would give help where it is most needed, and is the best way to grow the economy.

Read both parts of the source carefully. You could underline key points. You are not expected to agree with everything from either viewpoint, though you must reach a conclusion.

Examine whether each argument is supported with evidence or is simply an assertion. Evaluate **both** views and decide which arguments are more convincing.

The viewpoint that Labour is less radical than public opinion is supported by evidence of two polls.

Identify weaknesses in the reasoning in either of the arguments. For example, the claim that borrowing as a policy is not the solution is not supported with evidence.

Identify areas of both disagreement and agreement. For example, both argue that low interest rates and borrowing will not solve the UK's economic problems. They disagree on what should be done about Corporation Tax but recognise its importance in encouraging trade.

Read the questions on the next page. You should answer these using evidence from the source and your own opinion.

Practice Source D questions 2

Practise for **Paper 1, Section D** with these exam-style **short** and **extended writing** questions based on Source D on page 77. Example answers are provided (page 131 forward).

Guided

Study Source D on page 77 about whether taxes should be cut, then answer these questions.

Which of these does Owen Jones believe?   **(1)**

☐ **A** The media thought that Labour's tax plans were not severe enough.

☐ **B** Cutting the rate of Corporation Tax would harm UK overseas trade.

☐ **C** Increased tax on the rich would not harm the UK's economic recovery.

☐ **D** Public opinion showed concern that Labour's tax plans were unfair.

Which of these does Fraser Nelson believe?   **(1)**

☐ **A** High tax rates put more pressure on wealthy people than on those who have average incomes.

☐ **B** Low interest rates on mortgages have made it easier for many young people to buy houses.

☐ **C** The Bank of England was correct when it decided to cut interest rates and increase borrowing.

☐ **D** Tax cuts for the poorest in society have been proved in the past to help economic recovery.

Analyse Source D and identify **two** points on which both writers agree.   **(2)**

1 ....

....

....

2 ....

....

....

Short answer questions

Your responses to the **short answer questions** should help you when you answer the long answer question.

For these multiple choice questions, identify where in the source each of these ideas is mentioned, and eliminate answers before selecting the correct one.

The correct answer may not be stated directly in the source. You may need to infer it by analysing the statements in the passage.

In 'analyse' questions you need to get below the detail to understand the principles about which the writers are arguing. They may see the same problem but propose different solutions.

Long answer questions

For this **long answer extended writing** question, you must examine both arguments, analyse the evidence provided and decide which of them is, for you, the most credible. Provide a well-reasoned conclusion. Use a separate piece of paper to answer this question.

Guided

Which writer do you agree with more? Explain your answer, referring to the arguments made in both parts of the source.   **(12)**

Practice linked theme question

Practise for **Paper 1, Section D** with this **linked theme** exam-style question relating to citizenship issues and debates, and **two linked areas of content** from Themes A–C.

- -

Guided

'Scotland and Wales are more democratic than England.' How far do you agree with this view? Give reasons for your opinion, showing that you have considered different views on the topic.

In your answer, you could consider:
- the impact on identity of the UK being comprised of four countries
- the concept of representative democracy.   **(15)**

....
....
....
....
....
....
....
....
....
....
....
....
....
....
....
....
....
....

Read this **linked theme** question and identify the key words. The question is not asking if the countries are democratic. The question is asking **how far** Scotland and Wales are more democratic than England. The bullets prompt you to link with Theme A and Theme B.

Consider the following in your answer:
- How the identities of Wales and Scotland compare with England in relation to individual identity, and the location of the Westminster Parliament. What does this mean for democracy?
- 'Representative democracy' is a system where the people choose representatives to represent their views in government. It contrasts with direct democracy where rules are decided by a direct vote of all the people. Consider how far this varies between the three countries.
- Reasoned arguments showing breadth and depth. Give a convincing and sustained analysis of views on **both** sides of the argument. Reach a justified conclusion supported by your evidence.

Continue your answer on a separate piece of paper.

Citizen participation

Citizens can use their power and influence when they participate in and contribute to society, politics and democracy in the UK. There are opportunities for direct and indirect action, holding those in power to account, and contributing to wider public life. There may also be barriers to participation.

Opportunities for participation

Democracy means 'rule by the people'. A healthy democracy requires people to get involved in their communities, society and politics. People can get involved in:

- **politics** by voting or campaigning on a local, national or global issue.
- **the local community** by volunteering for local charities.
- **the wider community** by involvement in charities to improve health or campaign for justice and equality.
- **serving in society** such as a magistrate.

Barriers to participation

Barriers to participation in the community, society and politics include:

- **busy lives** or lack of time from working long hours or childcare.
- **a lack of interest** (apathy) about politics or community issues, feeling there is no point as it makes no difference.
- **a lack of awareness** and education on how to exercise power and influence.
- **worry about process** or the impact of their position in society on others.

Contributing through direct and indirect action

Direct action is when people try to achieve political goals themselves, e.g. through protests.

Indirect action is when people try to influence politicians to act for them, e.g. using petitions. Both methods contribute to the political process and hold those in power to account.

Examples of direct citizenship action	Examples of indirect citizenship action
Join or start a campaign, march, demonstration, protest.	Join a political party, vote in elections and referendums, stand for election as a councillor or MP.
Boycott companies or countries in protest of their actions or policies, or go on strike.	Lobby politicians or join a pressure group that tries to influence policy on a particular cause, or an interest or advocacy group.

Contributing to wider public life, including volunteering

People's reasons for getting involved in communities, society and politics include:

- concern about making a difference, e.g. for environmental or local issues
- influence from personal experience, or from parents or friends who already participate
- influence from cultural background or religion, believing it is their duty to help others
- ambition, such as making a career in politics or developing skills
- the desire to improve the community by completing work that otherwise is not done.

Now try this

Suggest **two** methods, one direct and one indirect, that a group wishing to make a difference to levels of child poverty in their town could use to help them achieve their goals.   (2)

Voter participation

A number of measures, including 'digital democracy' and use of social media are being developed by government as a means to improve voter engagement and political participation.

practical obstacles such as difficulty getting to a polling station due to lack of time, or disability

Why some people don't vote or participate in politics

they feel their vote will not make a difference

they are not interested in politics, and think it is nothing to do with them

they do not know or understand enough about the issues

they think the parties and candidates are all the same, and only in it for themselves

Improving voter engagement

Here are **six** possible solutions that may increase voter engagement.

1. Make voting compulsory, with fines for those who fail to vote.
2. Increase face-to-face meetings between candidates and voters.
3. Improve citizenship education for young people.
4. Change the first-past-the-post system so every vote counts.
5. Allow voting across the weekend.
6. Place polling stations at work or stores so it is convenient to vote.

Digital democracy

Digital democracy involves the use of online technology to engage voters with election campaigns and make them more likely to vote.

👍 Voting at home or on a mobile phone is easier and more accessible than going to a polling station. This is known as 'e-voting'.

👎 Very tight security is needed to prevent voter fraud or hacking of the process.

Voting via the internet (e-voting) could help increase voter engagement.

Improving political participation through social media

Parties increasingly use email, and platforms such as Facebook and Twitter to send messages.

👍 Messages can be targeted to particular voters.

👍 Getting page 'likes' and shares helps spread the party's message.

👍 Social media also allows parties to pick up on issues that are important to voters, which can help them direct their campaigns.

👍 Voter turnout rose in the last general election, and some believe that social media helped to engage young voters, who voted in higher numbers than previously.

👎 Politicians need to be careful about how they use social media, for example in 2014, Labour MP Emily Thornberry resigned from the shadow cabinet after tweeting a picture of a house covered in England flags, as some felt that she was mocking working-class voters.

👎 There are concerns about sites putting out 'fake news' that confuses voters, which could turn them off politics.

Now try this

Explain **two** ways in which political parties could encourage disenchanted electors to vote. **(4)**

81

Participation outside the UK

There are key differences in how citizens can and cannot participate in politics in political systems outside the UK. The examples below compare one **democratic** and one **non-democratic system.**

Democracy around the world

There are many democratic countries in the world, but also countries that lack some or all democratic features.

- Norway was ranked as most democratic nation by *The Economist*'s Democracy Index 2017. It was followed by Iceland, Sweden, New Zealand and Denmark. The UK was ranked at 14.

- North Korea was ranked as one of the five least democratic countries. The other four were the Democratic Republic of Congo, Central African Republic, Chad and Syria.

Democratic features

Democratic features reflected in *The Economist*'s Democracy Index study include:

- ✓ free and fair elections
- ✓ governmental checks and balances
- ✓ citizen inclusion in politics
- ✓ citizen support for the government
- ✓ freedom of expression for citizens.

Features of a democratic system (e.g. Norway)	Features of a non-democratic system (e.g. North Korea)
Most adult citizens can vote – registration to vote is automatic	No genuine elections – people can only vote for local officials, and most ballots only contain one candidate. National leaders are not elected
Most adult citizens can stand for election	The country's leader is a dictator who decides everything
Participation in elections is high and seen as a civic duty	There is no rule of law
Politicians are seen by voters as normal people, not as an out-of-touch elite	Kim Jong-un took over as ruler in 2011 from his father, who in turn took over from his father. He will be Supreme Leader for life
There is a wide range of parties that often cooperate in coalitions – this is called pluralism	The Workers' Party of Korea is the only party allowed and exercises direct control over all candidates in rigged elections
Elections are free, fair and open	The military is central to North Korea's politics
Anyone can join or form political parties and pressure groups	There are no opportunities to legally take part in any political activity that is not approved by the state
Freedom of expression is highly valued	Criticism of the government is likely to mean being sent to a prison camp
The media are free to express any view they want	There is no free media

Now try this

Explain **one** reason why elections in a one-party state such as North Korea are not truly democratic.

(2)

Groups in democratic society

Different organisations play a role in providing a voice and support for different groups in society. These include public institutions, public services, interest and pressure groups, trade unions, charities, and voluntary groups.

Public institutions and services

Public institutions include schools and universities, libraries, hospitals, and the courts. **Public services** include police, fire and ambulance services.

- They are funded by the state through people's income tax and National Insurance.
- They are usually staffed by paid workers.
- Government offers them to support citizens in their everyday lives, for example, the NHS ensures all citizens have access to healthcare that is free at the point of use.

Charities and voluntary groups

Voluntary groups and **charities** allow citizens to volunteer their time and skills. For example, standing up for justice and equality with Amnesty International or supporting people and raising funds as part of Asthma UK.

- They work to support causes or groups in society and are non-profit making.
- They aim to raise awareness and funds for their cause in order to improve conditions, eliminate disease or create social change.

Interest and pressure groups

People who belong to **interest groups** share a common interest that may be political or not, and can promote their ideas in many ways. **Pressure groups** are often interest groups that put pressure on government to adopt policies that help the issues they care about. Groups may be local, national or international. They may represent a cause or a section of society.

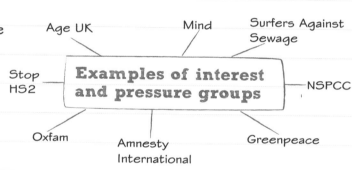

Age UK — Mind — Surfers Against Sewage — Stop HS2 — **Examples of interest and pressure groups** — NSPCC — Oxfam — Amnesty International — Greenpeace

- Thousands of pressure groups represent a huge number of causes that give people a voice, helping government get a better idea of public opinion.
- Many are voluntary organisations, though some do have paid staff.
- Charities often act as pressure groups for a cause in their area of focus.
- They use direct or indirect methods to try to change government policy, influence public opinion, or change the way that private companies operate.
- They hold government to account by spreading power and influence in society.
- Insider pressure groups are ones that government consults for expert information, such as the British Medical Association. Their closer ties with government may make them more influential.

Trade unions

Trade unions act on behalf of workers such as teachers, doctors, train drivers and shop workers. They give workers a voice and represent their interests to employers and in the democratic process. For example:

- they help to protect workers' rights and campaign to improve pay and conditions
- they use collective bargaining to negotiate with employers on behalf of members
- they can represent a worker at a tribunal if there is a dispute with the employer.

Now try this

Give **two** ways in which groups in a democratic society can influence the decisions of the government.   (2)

Citizens working together

Citizens can work together or through groups to change or improve their communities. This can be through actions to **address public policy**, **challenge injustice**, or **resolve a local community issue**. Here are **two** different examples.

Working together to use power and influence

It is much easier to make change or improve society by working together.

✓ When citizens pool their efforts, they can increase their power and influence on politicians and public opinion.

✓ If public opinion is behind an action, the government is more likely to pay attention. Politicians need to listen to citizens in order to win votes and stay in power.

National campaign

Open Britain was set up to challenge the UK's departure from the EU, connecting UK grassroots supporters to address public policy.

- It campaigned against a 'hard' or 'no deal' Brexit with a belief it would damage the British economy and leave people worse off, and also harm the UK's relations with Europe.

- It set out to hold government to account for its policy on leaving the EU, arguing for a 'people's vote' on the final Brexit deal.

- Members argued that a new referendum would show the public supported their position.

- The impact of the group can be judged in light of Brexit outcomes.

Local campaign

Hands Off HRI was set up to stop the closure of Huddersfield Royal Infirmary.

- This was a grassroots campaign that organised mass demonstrations, lobbying of politicians and fund-raising in support of these actions.

- They sought a judicial review of the government's decision to close the hospital. The judge upheld the campaign's view that closure was not supportable.

- The campaign succeeded. The Health Secretary at the time said closure of the hospital was not in the people's interests.

Citizens can change or improve their communities through working together or in groups, taking action to **address public policy** such as a national campaign around Brexit, to **challenge injustices** such as homelessness, or **resolve a local community issue** such as campaigning to keep a hospital open.

Now try this

Suggest, using an example, **one** way in which citizens can work together to change or improve their communities.

(2)

Protecting workplace rights

Trade unions are associations of workers who, as with staff associations and tribunals, protect and support the rights of people in the workplace.

Origin of trade unions

The industrialisation of Britain started in the late 18th century. It grew quickly in the 19th century as people moved to cities where new mills and factories changed the structure of society and the economy. Workers were grouped in bigger numbers and then challenged low wages and poor conditions, though until 1824 associations of workers were banned.

Timeline of trade unions

1824: The Combination Acts were repealed and unions began to grow

1868: The Trades Union Congress (TUC) was set up and helped get a change in the law

1871: Trade Union Act 1871 meant that unions were protected by law

1880s: 1m members fought for rights and improved pay and conditions

1900: Unions helped set up the Labour Party, to get workers represented in Parliament

20th century: Workers enjoyed a better standard of living and more secure employment

1979: Numbers grew to 13.2m, then new laws restricted union powers.

Trade unions today

Trade unions still maintain and improve conditions of employment through collective action, although anti-union laws brought in by the governments of Margaret Thatcher reduced the power and numbers of the unions to 6.2m by 2017. Reduced numbers reflect:

- a decline in Britain's heavy industry and a growth in the 'gig economy' of zero-hour contracts

- changes in the economy which led to years of reduced public spending and fewer public sector workers. Many union members are older.

Rights in the workplace

All workers are entitled to the following rights.

- **A contract of employment,** setting out job expectations, pay and terms.

- **At least national minimum wage,** with laws setting out the lowest wage.

- **Protection from discrimination** on grounds of ethnicity, age, gender, sexuality and disability set out by the Equality Act 2010.

- **Higher national living wage** for workers over the age of 25, since 2016.

- **Health and safety,** with laws for a safe working environment.

Protecting and supporting workers

Staff Associations carry out a similar role to Trade Unions (e.g. doctors belong to the British Medical Association) and they uphold rights in **three** key ways:

1. **Negotiation** with employers to improve pay and conditions (collective bargaining). A strike may be called if negotiations fail, with all members influencing the decision.

2. **Representation** of workers' interests to government to affect policy, to employers in relation to rights, disputes and redundancy, and to **tribunals** (page 59).

3. **Support** of members through education and training, or giving financial help if a member has a medical or financial crisis. Some unions support the Labour Party with donations.

Now try this

Explain **two** reasons why trade unions are still relevant today.   **(4)**

Democracy and the media

The media has a role in influencing and informing the public, reporting news accurately, investigating issues and exposing problems in the public interest. It also scrutinises government and those in power, holding them to account for their actions. A **free press**, which means that media can report without government control or restrictions, is important in a democracy.

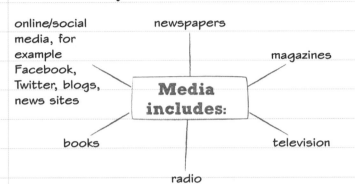

online/social media, for example Facebook, Twitter, blogs, news sites

newspapers

magazines

Media includes:

books

television

radio

Freedom of expression

Freedom of expression is in Article 19 of the Universal Declaration of Human Rights. Media have an important role in a democracy, which requires a free, fair and open flow of information so that:

- citizens know what is happening in society and make informed voting decisions
- citizens can hold the powerful to account.

Limiting freedom

Governments might sometimes need to limit freedom of the press through censorship, for example, to protect national security or to maintain public order.

Influencing and reporting

Accurate reporting is crucial in a democracy, which requires citizens to be well informed. There is a debate over how far the media:

- **informs** the public accurately through reporting facts (true whoever says them)
- **influences** the public about what to think through reporting opinions (personal, subjective viewpoints that may be biased) as if accepted facts.

Investigating and scrutinising

Reporting in the public interest helps ensure those with power such as politicians and big businesses cannot do whatever they like, as they must be seen as honest.

Media have a key role:

- to **investigate** issues and **expose** problems that are in the public interest
- to **scrutinise** (examine carefully) the government and those in power, holding them accountable.

Media and democracy

A good example of why a free press is important in a democracy is the media investigation and exposure of MPs' expenses claims scandal in 2009.

- It was in the public interest as MPs are elected to serve society and to only use taxpayers' money on expenses that help them do their jobs.
- It was discovered that some MPs were claiming expenses for things thought unnecessary or greedy. Many examples of false accounting were also found, and cases of tax evasion.
- The media investigations brought such MPs to justice and brought about a change in rules about what could be claimed on expenses.

Now try this

Explain the difference between the media informing the public or influencing the public.   (4)

Media rights and regulation

The media have a right to investigate and report issues that are in the public interest. This is subject to respect for privacy and dignity, accuracy, regulation and censorship.

Rights of the media

Matters in the **public interest** are those that affect people's everyday lives, such as education and health.

- Freedom of expression is a human right protected in the Human Rights Act 1998.
- The media can criticise governments without fear of being prosecuted.
- The Freedom of Information Act 2000 gives media the right to access a lot of government and local authority information.
- The media can check that politicians and companies are not breaking the law or acting unethically.

Accuracy and respect in reporting

The media have a responsibility to accurately report what happens. If they make up stories to sell papers or defame people (damage their reputation) it undermines democracy. People must make judgements on correct information. Media investigations must respect and not undermine the right to privacy and dignity.

- A newspaper can be sued for the civil offence of **libel** if they **write** untrue things about people.
- People can sue the media for the civil offence of **slander** if the media **says** untrue things about them.

Role of the press regulator

While a free press is important in a democracy like the UK, regulation is also important to set out the media's responsibilities. For example:

- The BBC is governed by a Royal Charter. It has a responsibility to be impartial and a duty to inform, educate and entertain.
- The government officially recognises the Independent Monitor for the Press (Impress), which has a standards code for its members.

The Leveson Inquiry

The Leveson Inquiry followed criticism of the media for lack of respect for the family of the missing student, Milly Dowler, in 2002. The recommendations resulted in new forms of media self-regulation. Some media businesses set up their own self-regulator in 2014, the Independent Press Standards Organisation (IPSO) which drew up the Editors' Code of Practice. Others, such as the *Financial Times* and *The Guardian* chose to self-regulate instead.

Reasons why censorship may occur

Censorship may occur for **two** key reasons:

1. To protect national security, keeping sensitive information from enemies (e.g. military operations).

2. To protect people from harmful and offensive content. OFCOM's Broadcasting Code sets out to:

   - **protect children**, by age-related rating of films and games and through the TV watershed
   - **respect court case restrictions**, e.g. protect identities of children; prevent the media from interviewing jurors
   - prevent the promotion or glorification of terrorism
   - **protect people's rights, including celebrities**, to privacy and from insulting, abusive, discriminatory or threatening language that may cause alarm or breach the peace.

Now try this

Explain **two** reasons why the press might resist greater controls on their activities. **(4)**

Media and influence

The media can be used by groups or individuals and those in power to try and influence public opinion.

Influencing public opinion

Public opinion refers to the views people hold on issues that affect their lives and community. Politicians often use research such as opinion polls, surveys and focus groups to find out what the public think, and make policy that appeals to them, in order to win votes. Many things influence public opinion, such as world events, local events, and friends and family, but the media is one of the strongest influences.

Groups and individuals

Groups and individuals can use the media to attract attention to issues. This may influence those in power to listen to people's voices, and address popular issues in Parliament.

- **Groups** can carry out protests, stunts and demonstrations to attract media attention and influence public opinion.

- **Individuals** can write directly to newspapers or magazines to get their message across, or start their own campaign on an issue to attract media attention.

- **Online methods** such as websites like change.org or 38 Degrees are increasingly used as a means for citizens to take action by starting and signing online petitions. A traditional media outlet might pick up and promote the issues, affecting public opinion.

A group of teenagers protest against the closure of local playing fields. Closure of playing fields and children's playgrounds as a result of cuts to local councils' budgets has attracted media attention and influenced public opinion.

Government and those in power

Government itself is concerned about shaping public opinion so that it is favourable to the government and its policies.

- Political parties employ 'spin doctors'; these are media experts who tailor their message so that it is more effective in influencing voters.

- Politicians also use experts to style their clothes and hair to make them seem more appealing when appearing in the media.

- At election time, parties are allowed to advertise on TV using party political broadcasts. These are basically long advertisements that deliver their key messages.

Influence through social media

Government and opposition parties are increasingly using social media to reach the public with their messages.

- Facebook 'likes', and shares and retweets on Twitter can help a message to spread widely, and can potentially influence many people. For example, over 216,000 people 'like' the UK Government's Facebook page.

- People regularly use their phones to access news media, and fewer people are now reading traditional newspapers.

- Many MPs effectively use blogs and social media profiles to promote their policies and let voters know what they are doing about important issues.

Now try this

Explain what is meant by public opinion, with **one** reason to say why it is important.   (2)

The UK and Europe

The UK's power and influence with the rest of the world includes roles and relations with the rest of Europe such as the European Union (EU) and the Council of Europe. There are differences between these organisations.

The European Union	The Council of Europe
Aims	
To encourage greater cooperation on issues such as peace, security, trade, the environment and social issues between member countries.	To promote human rights, democracy and the rule of law.
Set up	
Set up as part of the 1951 European Coal and Steel Community which became the European Economic Community in 1957.	Set up in 1949, following World War 2, to rebuild and maintain peace.
UK membership	
The UK joined in 1973 and in 2016 voted in a referendum to leave.	The UK was a founder member and has a permanent representative.
Consists of	
27 member countries, and includes different parts: • **The European Council** – made up of the heads of state of each member country; helps create EU law • **The European Commission**, which administers the EU and proposes new regulations • **The European Parliament**, elected by voters of all EU member states; discusses Commission proposals • **The Council of Ministers**, made up of one minister from each member country • **The Court of Justice of the EU** – each country has a judge that sits on cases involving EU law.	47 member countries and all EU members belong to the Council of Europe: • **The Secretary General** holds the role for 5 years • **The Committee of Ministers** has a minister for each state • **The Parliamentary Assembly** has parliamentarians from each member state, adopting resolutions and making recommendations to governments.
Relationship to laws and finances	
• EU law must be put in place in member countries, whose law must be consistent with EU law. • EU member states benefit economically from frictionless trade with other EU members.	• Cannot make binding laws but can enforce international agreements between members. • Developed the European Convention on Human Rights (EHCR) and runs the European Court of Human Rights, which enforces the ECHR. • The UK contributed around £32.8m in 2018.

Now try this

Give **two** functions of The Council of Europe.   (2)

Remember that: **The Council of Europe** is **not** formally part of the EU and has a different membership. **The European Council** is an institution that forms part of the **EU**, and is not the same as The Council of Europe.

EU membership benefits and obligations

Membership of the EU has benefits which include free trade, financial support for infrastructure and being part of a large market. Membership also has obligations (things that must be done) which include compliance with legislation and policies.

Benefits	Obligations
Free trade and being part of a large market	
• The EU is a free trade area in which member countries can trade goods without going through expensive border checks, with no charges when goods such as food and clothing cross borders. • Companies in member countries therefore have access to a single market of over 500 million people. • The competition within the single market helps keep prices low for consumers. • A common set of standards for goods means that shoppers and businesses know they are getting quality products.	• Membership of the single market and customs union obliges members to give preferential treatment to other EU members.
Financial support for infrastructure	
• EU regional funds provide financial support to help pay for regeneration of depressed areas and replace outdated infrastructure. • Working together to tackle environmental problems in the EU means creating a cleaner and greener environment.	• Member states have to pay into the EU to fund all its operations. This was around £13 billion from the UK in 2017.
Compliance with legislation and policies	
• The EU has contributed to peace within Europe since the 1950s, as war is much less likely between countries that are economically and culturally connected. • There is cooperation across borders on fighting crime, policing, and tackling terrorism. This helps to create a safer environment for citizens. • People who are citizens of EU member countries can live, work and study in any EU state. • European regulations help to protect workers' rights in all EU member states.	• Members of the EU enforce European Arrest Warrants for other EU countries, share information, and support sanctions agreed by the EU. • EU citizens can enter other member states to live, work and study. • EU law has primacy. This means that EU members must accept all EU laws and include them as part of their own country's laws.

Now try this

Give **two** benefits of being a member of the European Union. (2)

EU and Brexit

The UK left the the EU in 2020 following the 2016 referendum where the majority of voters chose leave. The impact of this can be assessed over time.

Impact of EU decisions

EU decisions had an impact on the UK (when a member state) such as setting standards for consumer rights, protecting the environment, and the free movement of citizens to live and work in the UK. Here are some examples.

Setting standards for consumer rights

When shopping in the EU, all citizens can expect the same rights under EU consumer law.

* Traders must provide clear information for consumers, with the total price including taxes. This includes online shopping and buying digital content.
* Consumers are protected by the **product liability directive**, which promotes health and safety standards. Companies producing goods are liable for harm their product causes.
* The Court of Justice of the European Union can act to protect consumers, who have less bargaining power than producers, and lack access to the same information.

Protecting the environment

The EU has laws on the environment.

* These protect the environment against acid rain and air pollution.
* EU rules make sure that member states aim to use more sustainable energy.
* EU agreements have seen sulphur oxide levels fall by 89% over the last 20 years.
* Over 100 laws have been developed by the EU which help the environment, for example, the Habitats Directive and the Birds Directive.
* 600 UK beaches now meet EU clean beach standards after EU laws prevented UK water companies from pumping raw sewage into the sea.

EU laws help protect the environment, which has an impact on the UK because the sea, wind and nature do not stop at national borders. Working together on environmental problems such as pollution is positive for the future of the planet – for people, wildlife and the oceans.

Free movement of citizens

Free movement of citizens is one of the four freedoms of the EU, established by the Maastricht Treaty in 1992. For example:

* Citizens of member states can work, study, live and retire in any EU nation.
* As a result of Brexit, UK citizens have lost freedom of movement within the EU. They can still travel and spend up to 90 days in the EU without requiring a visa.

Now try this

Using an example, explain **one** way in which EU membership has had a positive impact on the British environment.

(2)

The UK's role in the world

The UK has power and influence in the rest of the world through its relations with the United Nations, NATO, the Commonwealth, and the World Trade Organization.

The United Nations (UN)

The UN is an international organisation. It was set up by the international community in 1945 after World War 2 to avoid war and solve global problems through discussion.

- It includes 193 member countries.
- The UK joined in October 1945.
- The UK is one of five permanent members of the Security Council of the UN. This gives it a high degree of influence, as it can veto any resolution it disagrees with.

The UN General Assembly and agencies

The General Assembly of the UN is the UN's main body. Its role is to discuss important issues and make recommendations to solve them. The UN also has many agencies (sub-bodies) that help it to carry out these aims. For example:

- **The Human Rights Council** works to uphold human rights around the world.
- **The World Food Programme** helps get urgent humanitarian aid to people in disaster areas.
- **UNICEF** (the UN Children's Fund) works to help children all over the world, by putting pressure on governments to protect young people.

Functions of the UN

Key functions of the UN are to maintain international peace and security, protect human rights, deliver humanitarian aid, promote sustainable development and uphold international law.

The North Atlantic Treaty Organization (NATO)

NATO was set up in 1949 to defend Western Europe and the developed Western world against the threat of Soviet aggression.

- There were 29 members in 2018. The UK is one of the original members.
- It aims to guarantee freedom and security of members by military and political means and solve problems through negotiation, with military back-up if force is needed.
- It has been active in recent years in Afghanistan and Iraq as part of the international community's response to terrorism and the threat of weapons of mass destruction.

The Commonwealth

The Commonwealth is made up of countries once part of the British Empire (page 3).

- There are 53 member states.
- Queen Elizabeth is its head. In 2018, Prince Charles was appointed as her designated successor.
- It aims to promote economic, social and sustainable development, support democracy and peace, and protect the environment.

World Trade Organization (WTO)

The WTO is an international organisation that deals with trade between countries.

- Set up in 1995, it has has 164 members.
- The UK has been a member since 1995.
- It puts in place rules that govern how countries do business with each other.
- It tries to sort out disputes that arise when countries disagree about an issue.
- It aims to make trade more free, open and transparent, so that all the members can do business in an atmosphere of trust.

Now try this

Give **two** reasons why the UK still has influence in the modern world. (2)

Benefits and commitments

Benefits and commitments arise from the UK's membership of organisations such as the United Nations and its agencies, NATO, the Commonwealth, and the World Trade Organization. Here are some examples.

Benefits	Commitments
United Nations (UN)	
• The UK is a permanent member of the Security Council, which gives it a veto on any UN action. • The UK can count on assistance from other members in the event of a disaster. • The UK has access to financial help from the UN's World Bank agency. • UK citizens benefit because the UN's members take the protection of human rights seriously.	• The UK has to pay a membership fee. It is the fifth largest funder of the UN in general, and of its peacekeeping budget. • The UK has to contribute troops to peacekeeping missions around the world. • Being a permanent member of the Security Council is a big commitment. The UK has a key role in maintaining global peace, and in selecting the UN Secretary General, who heads the organisation.
North Atlantic Treaty Organization (NATO)	
• The UK's military can share expert knowledge with friendly countries, which makes success in conflict more likely. • Working with other like-minded countries improves the security of the UK as it can rely on their help if attacked.	• The UK is committed to send troops to serve under NATO command if another member is under threat as 'an attack on one is an attack on all'. • The UK is committed to spending 2% of its budget on funding NATO.
Commonwealth	
• The Commonwealth is a mutually-supporting community, so the UK benefits from strong relationships with other countries. • Pursuing shared goals makes the UK stronger and more likely to succeed in trade, climate change, and democracy. • The UK could rely on the support of other members if attacked, or if a disaster.	• The Commonwealth Charter commits the UK to uphold peace, democracy, human rights and protection of the environment. • The UK pays into the Commonwealth for the benefit of member nations. For example, in 2018 it announced a £500m commitment to tackle malaria, spent £212m on education of girls and committed £61m to tackle plastic waste.
World Trade Organization (WTO)	
• Trade barriers for UK companies are reduced with other members, so there are larger markets for UK goods. • Trade is smoother as members know the rules and stick to them. • It helps to resolve trade disputes. • All members get 'most favoured nation' status, so there can be no favouritism.	• Membership involves a commitment to avoid barriers to trade and to abide by WTO resolution of disputes. • 'Most favoured nation' status means the UK cannot be biased in favour of UK companies.

Now try this

Explain **two** benefits for the UK of belonging to the World Trade Organization (WTO).   **(4)**

Global responsibilities

The UK needs to balance its rights and responsibilities in challenging situations that involve global issues and human rights.

Human rights

All people are entitled to human rights, such as the right to life.

- Human rights are universal, which means that people of all ethnicities, genders and ages have them.
- They cannot be removed, even though they can be violated.
- The Universal Declaration of Human Rights (UDHR) sets out these rights.
- Most governments have signed the UDHR and have responsibility to respect the declaration.

Conflict situations

War is a constant problem for humanity. Fighting is always taking place somewhere in the world.

- Many conflicts are **civil wars**, fought between people of the same nationality in the same country. Such wars threaten the human rights of civilians caught up in the fighting, such as the civil war in Syria where thousands have been injured, died or become refugees.
- Other conflicts include threats to a **minority that is being persecuted**, such as the Rohingya people in Myanmar (Burma) because they are Muslims in a majority Buddhist country. Many have been killed, abused or become refugees.

Balancing rights and responsibilities

Human rights provide a framework for how to respond to global issues such as war. Human rights have a higher moral authority than laws passed by governments. This means that human rights come ahead of the right of a country to conduct its own affairs. Countries must balance self-interest with their responsibility to take human rights seriously.

Protecting human rights

The International Court of Justice and the International Criminal Court were set up to help enforce international humanitarian law on human rights in situations such as war.

Politicians, soldiers or civilians that violate human rights can be arrested and tried in these courts (see page 95).

Humanitarian intervention

The responsibility to protect human rights led to the development of the idea of humanitarian intervention by nations.

- This is where one country or a group of countries acts to tackle abuses of human rights in another country.
- For example, between 1998 and 2008 the UK and NATO intervened in Kosovo, part of the former Yugoslavia, to protect the human rights of civilians in the civil war.

Now try this

Identify **two** ways in which the human rights of ordinary citizens could be threatened by conflict situations.   (2)

International law

The role of international law in conflict situations is to limit the effects of armed conflict on civilians. International humanitarian law establishes the rules of war.

The Geneva Conventions

The 1949 Geneva Conventions are a set of key agreements in international humanitarian law.

- They are accepted by most countries in the world and set out the rules for the treatment of people in war. This includes prisoners of war, the wounded and sick, and civilians caught near war zones.

- For example, the use of biological and chemical weapons is forbidden, it is not permitted to kill an enemy who surrenders, the wounded and sick must be cared for by all sides, and civilians must not be attacked.

International humanitarian law

This refers to the rules agreed by different countries to protect the human rights of citizens in times of war.

- It aims to protect civilians and those no longer involved in fighting, such as prisoners of war.

- It tries to provide a way to deal with situations where human rights have been violated in conflict.

- A key principle of politics is national sovereignty, when a country has the right to decide what goes on within its borders, without outside interference. However, if a government is abusing its citizens, or cannot prevent abuse, then international humanitarian law permits outside organisations to take action to protect human rights.

International Criminal Court (ICC)

The ICC is a tribunal set up in 2002 and is based in The Hague, Netherlands.

- It is independent from the United Nations.

- It has 123 members, but some important countries, such as the USA, China and Russia are not signed up.

- It hears cases of serious crimes such as genocide, war crimes, and crimes against humanity.

- It acts only when national courts are unable to deal with a case, or when a case is referred by the UN or an individual country.

Judgments at the ICC attempt to find balance between punishment and restorative justice for those found guilty.

International Court of Justice (ICJ)

The ICJ ('World Court') is a United Nations organisation based in The Hague, Netherlands.

- It aims to settle legal disputes between member nations, concerning things like land or resources.

- It has 15 judges who are elected by the UN General Assembly and Security Council. These judges serve for 9 years.

- Only states can bring cases, not individuals, companies or other organisations. This makes it difficult for persecuted minorities in a state to have their case heard.

- Permanent members of the UN Security Council can avoid the ICJ by adopting a UN resolution.

- Countries who are ruled against do not have to accept the ruling as they are sovereign and cannot be forced to comply.

Now try this

Explain the difference between the International Criminal Court (ICC) and the International Court of Justice (ICJ).

(2)

Non-governmental organisations

Non-governmental organisations (NGOs) have a role in difficult global situations, which includes providing relief, protecting people at risk, and supporting development.

What NGOs are

NGOs are bodies that are not run by governments. They are independent from governments and from international organisations such as the UN and EU. NGOs:

- **might be charities** such as Oxfam or Save the Children
- **have experience** in human rights, disaster and crisis relief, the environment, and development
- **have clear humanitarian aims** to help those in need without benefits in return
- **are non-profit making** and raise money from appeals to the public to fund their activities
- **can work with governments**, who might use them worldwide and provide funding
- **do not take sides** in conflicts.

What NGOs do

NGOs protect people at risk and support development. Here are **five** examples.

1. **During natural disasters** such as floods, famines and earthquakes, charities such as Oxfam provide people with the skills to find clean water and food.

2. **When tackling disease** such as the outbreak of Ebola in Sierra Leone in 2015, charities use their expertise to help. For example, Save the Children trained community healthcare workers, funded by the UK Government's Department for International Development.

3. **When working with refugees**, NGOs are often involved. For example, the International Rescue Committee helps to resettle refugees in the United States.

4. **Where human rights need protecting**, NGOs campaign and advocate for human rights around the world by lobbying governments and raising awareness of violations. This includes NGOs like Amnesty International, and the International Red Cross.

5. **When improving conditions**, NGOs such as Water Aid with their expertise in the water industry, help provide technology and advice so that people in need have access to clean water and improved sanitation.

How resources impact on NGOs

NGOs lack the resources of government. This can limit them in achieving their aims.

Governments	NGOs
Can work together through international organisations such as the UN, NATO.	Largely depend on public support for funding through publicity events and demonstrations. If a cause is not popular, it can make their job difficult.
Have military personnel and can impose sanctions and send peacekeeping missions.	Can lose support and donations because of scandals. For example, some Oxfam relief workers in Haiti were accused of paying local women for sex after the 2010 earthquake.

Now try this

Using an example, explain the role of NGOs. (2)

UK's role in international conflict

Methods used when trying to resolve conflict in challenging global situations can include mediation, sanctions and force. Here are some examples where the UK has played a role.

Mediation

Mediation involves bringing together the different sides in a dispute. The aim is to find a negotiated solution to the conflict.

- A neutral third party (not involved in the dispute) helps the sides discuss the issues.
- All sides must be involved and listened to, otherwise mediation will not work.

For example, **the UK played a role** when Tony Blair was a Middle East peace envoy.

Sanctions

Sanctions are penalties for breaking rules in international situations. They put pressure on sides in a dispute. They target powerful people who can make a difference, to get them to alter their policies, end conflict and respect human rights. Sanctions could involve:

- not letting a country sell goods to other countries, thus causing economic hurt to effect change.
- a ban on selling military equipment to a country.
- expelling the country's diplomats from other countries.

For example, **the UK imposed sanctions** on Russia after its occupation of Crimea and its fighting in Ukraine, and on North Korea in response to its development of nuclear weapons.

Force

Force is a last resort, when mediation and sanctions have failed. Force could involve:

- direct intervention using the military.
- supporting other fighters in the conflict zone with equipment and expertise.
- setting up and enforcing a no-fly zone for another country's planes.

For example, **the UK directly intervened with its military** in Iraq in 2003, and used the Royal Air Force to **set up and enforce no-fly zones**, as part of operations with coalition forces in Libya.

Resolving conflict in Sierra Leone

In the 1990s, a civil war devastated the West African state of Sierra Leone, a former British colony. In keeping with the British Prime Minister Tony Blair's doctrine of humanitarian intervention, **the UK tried to resolve the conflict** through:

- sending soldiers and police officers to Sierra Leone as part of the UN mission set up to maintain the ceasefire.
- sending armed forces in May 2000 to evacuate foreign citizens as the Revolutionary United Front (RUF) advanced on the capital Freetown.
- working with the Economic Community of West African States (ECOWAS) in the 1999–2005 UNAMSIL operation to help stabilise the country by demobilising and disarming fighters from the war.
- training a new Sierra Leonean army, and a new civilian police force as part of the mission, in order to help the country defeat the RUF.
- sending about 900 British soldiers, permitted to use force, to help deal with a hostage crisis when rebels from the RUF captured UN peacekeepers. Mediation by the Liberian President Charles Taylor helped free the hostages.

Now try this

Explain **two** ways in which sanctions can be used to help resolve international conflicts.   (4)

Source A questions 1

Paper 2 is **1 hour 45 minutes** in total. You can revise for **Section A: Own citizenship action** focused on Theme E on page 126. In **Section B**, questions are focused on **Theme D: Power and influence** in relation to **others' actions**.

Paper 2 Section B Source A questions

The questions will be based on **Source A** which is about **citizenship actions carried out by other people**.

- The contexts for the actions may refer to any situation where citizenship action is relevant. You will need to understand, comment on and suggest actions.
- Questions will require short answers (see page 100) and a longer-answer (see page 101).
- The source may be in different parts.

Source A

Source A: 13th October 2014: Project Fields protest against building on green belt land

In 2013, <u>Labour-controlled Birmingham Council claimed 80,000 extra homes were needed by 2030.</u> Brownfield sites were inadequate, leaving no alternative to <u>building on greenfield sites</u> in leafy Sutton Coldfield. <u>Volunteers set up 'Project Fields' to organise protests. Through social media, they encouraged residents to object.</u>
In October 2014, the group <u>held a demonstration</u>. Led by Sutton Coldfield's Tory MP, Andrew Mitchell, <u>hundreds of people walked the perimeter of the scheduled 1,000 acre site.</u>

Walmley and Minworth residents protest against proposals to build 6,000 homes on green belt land.

Mitchell <u>accepted the need for new houses</u> but <u>opposed the loss of greenfield sites.</u> He said the <u>council had ignored 5,863 letters of complaint</u> and urged the <u>marchers to attend the public inquiry.</u> He <u>promised to fight the proposal to the bitter end.</u>
Project Fields spokesperson Suzanne Webb said they had <u>tried to understand the council's plans, but the council had ignored their complaints. She begged for the green belt to be saved.</u>

 Read Source A on pages 98–99. Underlining key points in a source can help focus your answer, as shown here.

 The questions will require you to use your knowledge and experience of involvement in a citizenship action. Here, the focus is on an objection to plans to build on green belt land.

 You do not need to know the area where the citizenship actions took place. What is important is how well you understand what people did, what success they had and whether they achieved their main objective.

 Establish the information that any photos and captions give you.

 Note how the demonstrators involved their local MP as a figurehead to their actions.

Now read the next part of the source on page 99.

Source A questions 2

Source A starts on page 98 and continues below.

Source A

Source A: 21st April 2016: Public consultation on developer's plans

In 2016, the public inquiry <u>agreed the proposal from Birmingham Council to allow developers to build on green belt</u> land. <u>Immediately the council promised to meet residents to discuss the developers' plans</u>. Then, six weeks of public consultation began in September 2018 in an <u>atmosphere of anger and frustration. Work was due to start six weeks after the consultation ended</u>.

Fields near Sutton Coldfield where it is proposed to build 6,000 new homes

Accepting the inevitable loss of green belt, <u>protestors wanted to secure improvements to the plans</u>. Mr Mitchell <u>hoped the meetings would produce positive results</u>, saying that <u>Sutton Coldfield residents should have a major input into a development forced on them by the council</u>.

Project Fields organiser Suzanne Webb, <u>now a Conservative councillor, accepted that the plan would be carried out. She was glad that the developers would listen to residents and hoped for a positive response</u>. She urged <u>everyone to work together and turn a tragedy into something good. Project Fields had lost the main battle but could influence the result</u>.

The second part of the source tells you how the public inquiry rejected demands not to allow development on the green belt. It accepted Birmingham's claim that they needed this if they were to meet house-building targets.

The citizens' action failed in its main aim but they were invited to discuss the plans. They were angry with the outcome.

This picture was posted by the Project Fields campaign group. Consider why they posted it and what message it carries to the general public.

Citizens continued to work together to try and improve a plan they couldn't stop and that had been forced on them. Consider how far their actions were reasonable and balanced different citizens' needs.

Both parts of the source show emotional language used by Project Fields, such as 'tragedy', 'forced on them', 'leafy Sutton Coldfield'. Consider how this creates messages in the reader's mind about a viewpoint and to influence future action.

Now try this

From reading both parts of Source A, suggest **two** reasons why supporters of Project Fields could be described as people protesting with a mindset of 'not in my back yard'.

Short answer questions

In **Paper 2, Section B**, questions are focused on **Theme D: Power and influence: others' actions**. These questions relate to Source A on pages 98–99.

Paper 2 Section B Source A short answer questions

Some questions require short answers. Here are command words you might see:

- **which, give, identify, name:** where you give a point or example without further development.
- **explain:** where you make a point and then develop it to show your understanding.
- **suggest:** where you show your understanding when reasons are less clear cut.
- **analyse:** where you analyse sources to understand the arguments made.

Worked example

Study Source A (pages 98–99) before you answer this question. The source mentions a public inquiry and public consultation. Explain these terms. **(4)**

For each term you need to give a simple definition and then develop your answer in the context of Source A.

A public inquiry is an official hearing to examine evidence and investigate public concerns about an issue. The public can attend and contribute. Here it is about the proposal from Birmingham City Council to allow developers to build on green belt land.

A public consultation is a regulatory process for the general public to express their views on a proposal. It might include surveys, online engagement, talking with individuals and meetings. Here, the developers included an open meeting to find out what local people thought of their plans

The source shows the local MP played a leading role in the demonstration.

Suggest **two** reasons why he supported the objectors. **(2)**

'Suggest' tells you to work out two possible answers based on the source. You don't need to develop your answers.

1 It was political. He was a Conservative and the council was Labour.

2 He thought it was wrong to build on green belt land.

The context of the question is the MP so only answer in relation to the MP, not other people.

According to the source, the public consultation met in an 'atmosphere of anger and frustration'.

Using the source, analyse the reason for this. **(2)**

They believed the council had ignored their letters of complaint and were determined to build on the green belt whatever objections there were.

Analyse a valid reason and develop it into an explanation that relates to evidence in the source.

Now try this

Give **two** reasons why the council needed to build houses on green belt land, according to Source A.   **(2)**

Long answer question

You will be asked a question about Source A that focuses on the **actions of others** and requires a **longer answer** with more **detail**.

Paper 2 Section B Source A long answer question

You may be asked an **explain** question which requires a reasoned explanation that shows your understanding by justifying or examples. Make sure you:

- show detailed knowledge about the concepts, terms and issues relevant to the question.
- show good understanding of how these apply, by commenting about the actions in the context of the source and the question.

Worked example

Explain the methods used by 'Project Fields' to oppose Birmingham Council's proposal to release green belt land for house building. **(6)**

'Project Fields' encouraged residents to write to the council to voice their objections to the plan. This produced over 5,000 letters and showed the strength of opposition. They also used social media to draw attention to the proposal, build up opposition and encourage people to do something about it. When we used social media for our campaign, we found it produced a lot of interest and support.

They organised a responsible demonstration which attracted hundreds of demonstrators. They walked the perimeter of the land, which drew attention to its size. The photographs show the strength of feeling and how the green belt is needed for things like exercise and recreation. They involved the media to publicise the demonstration, and the source also mentions the use of social media as a means of publicity.

They involved a locally popular and well-known MP as a leading figure in the campaign. His comments provided soundbites for the media. It may be that he circulated his views in his newsletter to his constituents. In our campaign to stop congestion we got the help of our local councillor. He also used his newsletter to tell residents about the problem and ask for their support. As a prominent MP he was potentially in a position to influence the government.

Attendance and participation at the inquiry helped to make local people's objections known and tried to influence the inspector. The source shows them using emotive language to paint the council as an oppressive agency trying to force an unreasonable plan on people who didn't want it.

This question relates to Source A on pages 98–99. You are not expected to know anything about this campaign beyond what is in the source.

Apply your own experience of a citizenship action to the evidence in the source.

Develop detail related to the source rather than a general response. Do not copy out the source, but your answer must link to the actions described in it.

This focuses on relevant points in relation to the source, developing the detail. The question is about methods used to oppose development on green belt land, so what happened next is not relevant.

Now try this

Explain **two** reasons why it was important for the organisers of the protest to involve their local MP.

Practice Source A questions

Practise for **Paper 2, Section B, Power and influence: the actions of others,** with these exam style questions. Read **Source A** below, then answer the questions on pages 103–104.

Guided

Source A: Community action to restore Jones Wood

Jones Wood is an ancient woodland on the outskirts of a town near Birmingham. It has over 420 years of continuous documented use as woodland and is now a protected area. It covers 2.4 hectares (6 acres) and consists mainly of oak and birch with some beech and sycamore. During the last 50 years it has been neglected and fallen out of use.

In 2014, local residents decided to recover the woodland and restore it to community use, setting up the Friends of Jones Wood. They have raised funds, cleared debris, constructed new paths and bridges, planted hundreds of trees and bulbs, and taken measures to improve safety.

Jaguar Land Rover (JLR) is a major local employer. It encourages staff to do community work by paying them for 16 hours annually to devote to charitable work. In 2017, 25 JLR employees worked for two days with the Friends of Jones Wood and council employees. They helped prepare the woods for community use by laying paths, clearing trees, erecting notices, repairing gates and planting 300 trees. JLR donated £3,000 towards the Friends' community work and a large container for storing equipment.

Jones Wood, Walmley, is now a haven of tranquillity in the urban environment. Birds, and other wildlife, are returning.

As well as regularly working weekends, the Friends have arranged activity days, including an Easter egg trail for children. In December 2017, they held a Christmas community event. The woods were illuminated, music and entertainment was provided, and food stalls and a Santa's Grotto set up. They raised money for ongoing work and to make local residents aware of the treasure house on their doorstep.

The local MP acknowledged the Friends' inspirational activist spirit for their tireless work to bring life back to this forgotten enclave. Jones Wood, after years of neglect, is growing in popularity with local residents.

Read the source carefully. You could underline key points. You must demonstrate detailed knowledge about the citizenship concepts, terms and issues relevant to this source.

Establish what the source tells you about the action. For example, why local volunteers decided to set up the Friends of Jones Wood, and what the volunteering work involved.

Establish who the action involved. For example, alongside local volunteers, why a company like Jaguar Land Rover involved themselves in this activity.

Establish what the photo and caption tells you about the impact of the action on the community and the environment.

Consider how the community action is funded. For example, any contribution from employers or fundraising events.

Consider the steps the volunteers took to build up support in the local community.

Now answer the questions on pages 103–104.

Practice short answer questions

Practise for **Paper 2, Section B: Power and influence: the actions of others,** with these exam-style short answer questions based on Source A on page 102. Example answers are provided (page 131 forward).

- -

Guided

Study Source A on page 102 before you answer these questions.
Explain **two** ways that volunteers and the Friends of Jones Wood have tried to improve safety. **(4)**

1 ....
....
....
2 ....
....
....

> Remember that your answers must be based on the source.

> You should make two clearly separate points about safety. Each point you make should be developed.

Suggest **two** reasons why the wood is growing in popularity with local residents. **(2)**

1 ....
....
....
2 ....
....
....

> You should suggest two different ways, using evidence from the source. You do not need to develop your answer.

According to the source, JLR (Jaguar Land Rover) has provided financial and personnel support.
Analyse why JLR has become actively involved in the renovation of the woodland **(2)**

....
....
....

> The source tells you about JLR's involvement but does not say why. You need to work this out from clues in the source like 'local' and 'charitable'.

> You only need to make a single point but your analysis has to be developed with an explanation.

Practice long answer question

Practise for **Paper 2, Section B: Power and influence: the actions of others,** with this exam-style long answer question based on Source A on page 102. Example answers are provided (page 131 forward).

Guided

Study Source A on page 102 before you answer this question. Source A shows that the community action to restore Jones Wood involved the Friends of Jones Wood and the support of other agencies, organisations and individuals. Explain why the Friends needed this support.   **(6)**

....

....

....

....

....

....

....

....

....

....

....

....

....

....

....

....

....

....

....

....

....

Show that you understand the source and can apply your knowledge and understanding of citizenship concepts, issues and terms to answer this question.

Consider the following in your answer:

- Evidence from the source and your own experience of citizenship actions. Do not write a general answer which could relate to any action.
- Who became involved, and why. Look for evidence of how the Friends relied on support from others.
- What the Friends might have achieved if they did not have help, especially from JLR.
- What the community activities involved.

Multiple choice questions

In **Paper 2, Section C**, questions are focused on **Theme D: Power and influence**. The final linked theme question will link content from Theme D with one of Themes A to C of your course.

Paper 2 Section C short answer questions

Some questions are multiple choice or require short answers. You will need to show or apply knowledge and understanding of citizenship concepts, terms, issues and actions. Here are command words you might see:

- **which, give, identify, name:** where you give a point or example without further development.
- **explain:** where you make a point and then develop it to show your understanding.
- **suggest:** where you show your understanding when reasons are less clear cut.

Worked example

Each of the following is true of pressure groups **except:**   (1)

☐ **A** more people belong to pressure groups than are members of political parties

☐ **B** pressure groups generally address issues that politicians often ignore

☐ **C** pressure groups can raise issues of immediate importance with politicians

☒ **D** most of the income received by pressure groups is taxed as a charitable gift

> You should understand that a pressure group puts pressure on government to adopt policies within the areas and causes pressure groups care about. A–C are true of them, and D is not.

Which of these is a public institution?   (1)

☐ **A** Harrods department store

☒ **B** The Queen Elizabeth NHS Hospital

☐ **C** The National Trust

☐ **D** Sadler's Wells theatre

> You should know that a public institution is an organisation provided by the government for the public to use as opposed to a privately run institution.
> Each of these serve the public but only the hospital (NHS) is provided by the government.

Two roles of a free press in a democracy are to: (2)

☐ **A** loyally support the elected government

☐ **B** provide newspapers for free

☐ **C** expose minority groups which fail to conform

☒ **D** try to prevent the general public from being misled

☒ **E** draw attention to wrong doing and injustice

☐ **F** support movements seeking to usurp power

> The key words in the question are 'free press' and 'democracy'. The contrast is with a press which is government controlled.
> Answers A, C, and F might be true of a controlled press in a dictatorship but do not fit with the key words.

Now try this

A group dedicated to using peaceful means to prevent badger culling is an example of a: (1)

☐ **A** single-issue group   ☐ **C** promotional group

☐ **B** multi-cause group   ☐ **D** human rights group

Short and long answers

Some questions require short answers and one needs a longer answer focused on **Theme D: Power and influence.**

Worked example

Using an example, explain one reason why the press may be censored by the government in peace time. **(2)**

For example, when spies are on trial. This is because information spies give in a trial may threaten security.

Give **two** different ways the UK has helped to deal with international disagreements. **(2)**

1 Acting as a mediator between enemies.

2 Using sanctions to show disapproval.

Explain **two** ways in which citizen participation in politics is different in democratic and non-democratic societies. **(4)**

1 A democracy has free elections where all eligible citizens can choose the government. Non-democratic states do not hold free votes and citizens have no political power.

2 In a democracy you can lobby your MP to try and influence them. In non-democracies this is often not possible or allowed, as those in charge do not listen to the people.

Explain the main functions of the Council of Europe and the European Parliament. **(6)**

The Council of Europe is an intergovernmental body with main functions that promote human rights, democracy and the rule of law. It is not part of the European Union. It developed the European Convention on Human Rights (ECHR) and runs the European Court of Human Rights which enforces the ECHR. There are 47 member states with benefits and demand on its members. For example, it can enforce international agreements between members, and it demands a financial contribution. The UK is a main contributor, paying over £32m in 2018.

The European Parliament is part of the European Union. Its main function is to discuss draft laws put forward by the European Commission, and enforce EU regulations. It can call for new policies to be launched, or for changes to existing ones. Members are elected by voters across all EU member states so they can represent the interests of the constituents in their country and make sure voters' voices are heard.

> If you are asked for an example, you must give both a point **and** an example.

> If you are asked for two different ways, make sure your points are **separate** and **clearly different**.

> Remember to look at the command words and the number of marks available. Here, you need to explain 'two ways'. For each way, make a point and then develop it.

> For the long answer question such as the below, make sure you can explain the roles and functions of all the international organisations named in Theme D of your course. Be prepared to answer a question based on two named international organisations. You must refer explicitly to both identified organisations.

Now try this

Suggest **three** reasons why Trade Unions were set up. **(3)**

Reasoned argument question

One question in **Paper 2, Section C** will give a **viewpoint** based on **Theme D: Power and Influence** and ask for a **reasoned argument for** and **against** it. No conclusion is required.

> **Paper 2 Section C Reasoned argument question**
> Answers should include:
> - convincing and sustained analysis of relevant viewpoints on both sides of the argument.
> - an evaluation with reasoned, coherent arguments, showing good breadth and depth.

Worked example

'Pressure groups have too much freedom to impose their ideas on other people'.
Write reasoned arguments to support and oppose this argument.   **(10)**

Consider how this answer puts forward reasoned and balanced arguments that both **support** and **oppose** the argument with **specific evidence** to support points for both sides.

Pressure groups are groups of people with similar views who campaign for change. They are not political parties but exist to influence decision makers. For example, they may try to improve street lighting or stop fracking. Pressure groups operate in different ways, for example lobbying, campaigning or using the media.

Demonstrations are legal if they act within the law but action that affects the public should be controlled. Extreme action may put off the public and decision makers. Protests should not have freedoms that block the public's way, trespass or damage property.

Pressure groups may get more attention than their numbers justify. 'Fathers 4 Justice' has sometimes trespassed to attract attention, which is illegal even if the campaign is justified. Pressure groups are entitled to their views but should recognise they are not shared by all and it is unfair to force them on others. They can influence decision makers too much, especially if they

are well-financed or have good media skills. Campaigns should be peaceful and within the democratic process. Elected councils and governments who take decisions should not suffer unreasonable pressure.

However, pressure groups do show that democracy works, making decision makers accountable with controls on what they do. They raise public awareness and may have specialist knowledge. For example, 'Ash' against smoking in public places has benefited health and the Suffragettes resulted in votes for women. In a democracy everyone is entitled to an opinion and to be heard. Pressure groups make this possible. Freedom to take action is essential for democracy and should be defended.

Most pressure groups are law-abiding and use their freedom to demonstrate, protest and campaign peacefully and legally. Pressure groups should have the same freedom as everybody else, but be equally subject to the same laws.

Now try this

Identify **three** advantages of having pressure groups in a democratic society.

Linked theme question 1

One question in **Section C** will **state a point of view** related to **Theme D: Power and influence** and ask you to explain **how far you agree** with it and come to a conclusion. You will need to **link content** from Theme D with one of Themes A to C.

Paper 2 Section C linked theme question

This question requires extended writing. You will need to:

- demonstrate analysis and evaluation in relation to the viewpoint, fully addressing both sides of the argument with breadth and depth.
- consider two linked areas of content including evidence and supporting examples.
- show clear judgment in reaching your verdict and expressing your opinion, supported by the evidence and examples you have provided.

Worked example

'NATO is a powerless and unnecessary expense that the UK can no longer afford.'

How far do you agree with this view?

Give reasons for your opinion, showing that you have considered other points of view.

In your answer you could consider:
- the role of NATO and the UK's relations with it.
- taxation and government spending.

(15)

Consider how this answer outlines the role of NATO and considers different points of view and not just one giving **specific evidence** and **examples**. Be familiar with the key concepts and terminology of the course. Here, the bullets link Theme D and Theme B.

Read the answer that starts on this page and continues on page 109.

NATO is a military alliance of 29 countries in Europe and North America, set up in 1949 to provide shared security against a Russian threat. It aims to guarantee freedom and security for members by military and political means, preferring to solve problems through negotiation if possible. The UK, a founder member, is the second largest contributor in financial and military terms.

NATO should be counted as a success because it has maintained peace in Europe since it was established. The only serious military threat to Europe since the 1950s was during the Balkan wars of the 1990s. NATO helped restore and maintain peace in this region by providing peace-keeping forces. It had previously helped UN forces maintain peace in Cyprus. Member nations are more secure because they can work together. They know that if they are attacked, they will receive political and military support from NATO.

NATO enables the military of each member state to share expertise and security information. This has worked, until the conflict between the Ukraine (an aspiring member since 2018) and Russia. The alliance means that each member will provide military help if another member is attacked. This means that any member can call on military forces and equipment far in excess of their own military services. This has given greater security to member states.

Linked theme question 2

The example **linked theme** question starts on page 108 and continues below.

Worked example

NATO not only protects European states. It has recently been active in the conflicts in Iraq and Afghanistan and has been part of the international communities' 'war against terror' and the search for 'weapons of mass destruction'. NATO has cooperated with other international organisations to maintain peace.

However, in recent years NATO has appeared powerless when faced with super-power hostility. It could not stop Russian aggression in the Ukraine or prevent the annexation of Crimea. This failure reflects on the organisation's aims. NATO's only effective power, short of open conflict, is the use of economic sanctions. These are ineffective against Russia. NATO's powerlessness is underlined by its failure to halt the civil war in Syria.

The UK has enjoyed peace for sixty years, but at a financial cost of an annual contribution to NATO of 2% of GDP. Unlike most member states, the UK has given this even during the last decade of austerity. Many ask if this commitment is justified when the NHS is crumbling through inadequate resources, education is starved of funds, and social welfare is underfunded. Many say payments to NATO should be cut to provide funds for UK services and avoid further tax rises.

NATO's existence is threatened by the erratic policy of President Trump who has threatened to quit unless member states pay a larger part of NATO's budget. If America pulls out, then NATO, which is already ineffective, may collapse. The UK certainly cannot increase the amount of taxpayers' money it gives to NATO.

NATO has been important in preserving peace in Europe but now it seems increasingly ineffective when faced with aggression. Expenditure is too high for member states, especially the UK, and it seems it can no longer provide the security Europe wants. Britain has an exaggerated sense of its strength and importance in international affairs, while our essential services face severe difficulties which can only be solved by massive investment. The government should pull out of NATO and concentrate on our own problems. NATO is a great idea, but it has outlived its usefulness. It is a luxury we can no longer afford.

 This develops and expands the answer, showing analysis of the viewpoint with sustained comment.

 Consider the other viewpoint. This is in agreement of the statement in the question, links to the second theme about taxation, and uses specific knowledge in support.

A question which asks 'How far' requires you to give a conclusion that is developed from the arguments and evidence you have considered. Make sure that you express an opinion. You don't have to agree or disagree completely with one view. You may find some good in different viewpoints. Here, the answer gives a conclusion that links the two themes together.

Now try this

'The UK needs to maintain its support for NATO in spite of the domestic demands on its finances.' Give **three** reasons which support this statement.

 This question asks for reasons that **support** the need for NATO. Do not focus on UK domestic needs.

Practice short and long answers

Practise for **Paper 2, Section C** with these exam-style questions based on **Theme D: Power and influence.**

Guided

Membership of the EU gives each of these, **except**:   (1)
- ☐ **A** Free trade with other member states
- ☐ **B** Access to the world's largest market
- ☐ **C** A single multi-nation armed force
- ☐ **D** Financial help to develop infrastructure

> You need to know about the benefits and obligations of membership of the EU (page 90).

Using an example, explain one restriction on what a free press can print.   (2)

....

....

....

> Include an explanation **and** an example.

Give **two** ways in which people in power can use the media to influence opinions.   (2)

1 ....

....

2 ....

....

> Your answer must relate to 'people in power' and not be too general a response.

Explain **two** reasons why the UK voted to leave the EU.   (4)

1 ....

....

2 ....

....

> Give two clearly different reasons. For each reason, make your point and then develop your point.

Explain the main roles of the United Nations and the World Trade Organization.   (6)

> For this longer answer question, you must explain **both** organisations (see pages 92–93). Use a separate piece of paper for your answer to this question.

Practice reasoned argument

Practise for **Paper 2, Section C** with this **reasoned argument** exam-style question based on **Theme D: Power and influence**.

Guided

'In a democratic society there should be few limitations on what the media can print, say or show.'

Write reasoned arguments to support and oppose this argument.   **(10)**

....

....

....

....

....

....

....

....

....

....

....

....

....

....

....

....

....

....

....

A **reasoned argument** question gives you a viewpoint based on Theme D. You need to put forward arguments that both **support** and **oppose** the argument. It is not enough just to side with one viewpoint of the argument. No conclusion is required.

Consider the following in your answer:

- Specific evidence and examples to support your points for both sides of the argument (see pages 86–88).
- The role of the media in a democratic society.
- Why limits exist for the media and whether these are too harsh or should be tightened up.
- Censorship.
- Debate about who regulates the media.
- Debate about what drives the media — accurate reporting or profit.

Continue your answer on a separate piece of paper.

Practice linked theme question

Practise for **Paper 2, Section C** with this **linked theme** exam-style question relating to **Theme D: Power and influence**. You will need to **link content** from **Theme D** with **one of Themes A–C**.

'Trade unions are more likely to improve working conditions in the UK than the government is.'

How far do you agree with this view?

Give reasons for your opinion, showing that you have considered other points of view.

In your answer you could consider:
- the role of trade unions
- why we need laws in society.

(15)

....

....

....

....

....

....

....

....

....

....

....

....

....

....

....

....

....

....

This linked theme question requires you to examine the role of government and unions in protecting and improving working conditions. The question links Theme D and the role of the trade unions with Theme A and why we need laws in our society.

Consider the following in your answer:

- Your understanding of the key concepts in the question. Note the importance of 'improve'. It means more than 'protect'.

- The historic reasons for the need for trade unions.

- Ways to support your argument with evidence and examples. Do not give a general answer about working conditions. Give a specific answer related to the question.

- Reasoned argument looking at both sides of the viewpoint. Remember that you must reach a justified conclusion.

Continue your answer on a separate piece of paper.

Your citizenship action

You will **plan**, **research** and **carry out** a citizenship action about an issue arising from your course. The action should make a **difference** for a particular community or wider society, locally, nationally or globally. Questions about your action are in **Paper 2, Section A**.

Stages of action

A citizenship action has **six** stages:

1. Identify an issue based on any aspect arising from your course (Themes A–D), form a team and carry out initial (secondary) research.
2. Undertake primary research.
3. Represent your own and different points of view.
4. Plan the action.
5. Apply skills of collaboration, negotiation and influence as you deliver the activity.
6. Critically evaluate your learning and the impact of the action.

Planning an outcome

Your citizenship action should have an outcome, using **one** of these approaches.

Either: Organise and deliver an event, meeting or campaign to advocate for your selected issue, problem, cause or social need. You should aim to argue a case that will raise awareness and commitment by informing, influencing and persuading your target audience.

Or: Organise and deliver a social action project, social enterprise or community action to raise awareness and commitment and create a social benefit (resources, support, advice or service) to benefit others.

For example, at a local takeaway, a group might raise awareness about local social problems using posters, photos and interviews with the manager and customers.

For example, a group might organise a campaign among students and parents to persuade school senior management and governors to make changes to the school uniform.

Forming a team

Show that you can work democratically and effectively in a team of two or more people.

Benefits of teamwork	Challenges of teamwork
👍 Sharing ideas and discussing actions to bring together different perspectives	👎 Too much time in discussion, arguing about what should be done, blurring aims
👍 Increasing the range of skills available by allocating work according to skills, and providing support and enouragement	👎 Some may dominate, find it difficult to compromise, not pull their weight or even drop out

Now try this

Explain how democratic your approach was when deciding what issue to address in your citizenship action.   (2)

Give **specific** details of your activities or discussions. Explain **why** your discussions were democratic, then develop the point.

Identifying an issue

Stage 1 of your citizenship action requires you to identify an issue based on any aspect arising in **Themes A–D** of your course, form a team and carry out initial (secondary) research.

Focusing your citizenship action

Do	Don't
👍 Be specific	👎 Be vague or general
👍 Show the link to the Theme in your course	👎 Forget to show the link to the Theme
👍 Choose an issue that involves 'action'	👎 Just invent 'knowledge'
👍 Choose a manageable topic	👎 Choose too big an issue
👍 Address all six stages of the action	👎 Choose something you can't evaluate

Choice of approaches

Approaches to citizenship actions may include:

- voluntary work
- involvement in community organisations
- participation in local or national politics
- organising campaigns or protests
- joining pressure groups.

Choice of methods

Methods for citizenship actions may include:

- public meetings, leaflets, newsletters
- use of the media and internet
- lobbying organisations or politicians
- petitions
- protests and demonstrations.

Use your knowledge and understanding from your course of the range of methods and approaches relevant to citizenship actions that can be used by individuals, groups, organisations and governments to address citizenship issues in society.

Worked example

In **no more than 20 words**, write the title of your citizenship action.

Example 1: To raise student awareness of disturbance caused to local residents by students at home time. (Theme A5)

Example 2: To organise a mock election to raise awareness among students of the nature of parliamentary elections. (Theme B2)

Example 3: To raise student awareness of differences between civil and criminal law. (Theme C3)

Example 4: To petition the council to address problems caused by congestion near the school. (Theme D1)

You should create a title for a citizenship action that interests you, and uses the skills of your team. These are only examples to give you the idea. Each of these titles:

- is no more than 20 words (as required in your exam) and is clearly linked to one of themes A-D of the course
- meets one of the two types of action and all six stages described for citizenship action (see page 113)
- has a clear outcome that can be assessed and is SMART (specific, measurable, achievable, realistic, timebound)
- explains the nature of the citizenship action and gives a focus to the work

Now try this

Explain **two** problems your team faced when choosing what citizenship action to take. **(4)**

Make two points and develop each point. Your answer **must** relate to your own experience and not be too vague or general.

Secondary research

Secondary research is required when preparing for your citizenship action and in planning to carry out primary research. Make sure you can explain what secondary research and secondary sources are and how they influenced the shape of your action.

Secondary research

Secondary research for your citizenship action involves gathering, analysing and using information from existing research. It can be called 'classroom research', as it uses printed materials and the internet. It should help guide your decisions on primary research (see pages 116–118).

Secondary sources

Secondary sources include:

- reports from public bodies, news and media
- information from NGOs and organisations
- opinion polls, statistics, data, textbooks, videos
- internet blogs and social media
- examples of previous citizenship actions.

Choosing secondary sources

Use secondary sources which are:

- **up to date** – so you have current contexts and the latest information to inform your action
- **unbiased** – so you have factual information that isn't just opinion
- **balanced** – so you can consider views and opinions to see contrasting sides of situations
- **relevant** – so you have something specific to say about your issue.

Purpose of secondary research

Secondary research helps you to:

- build up knowledge about your topic
- plan and modify your action
- refine your title
- decide on your proposed outcomes
- identify possible difficulties
- design your own research questions
- identify what further information you need.

Analysing research

When analysing research to see what you have learnt and what you still need to do, **three** key questions are useful:

1. Are your ideas about your chosen issue clear?
2. Do you need to modify your title, aims or method?
3. What must you do to achieve your outcome?

Worked example

Explain how **one** secondary source helped you plan your citizenship action. **(4)**

We used a report in the local paper about the noise students make when going home from school. The report said local people were unhappy with this. We decided to interview them about why they were unhappy. We decided to talk to students who went home that way and get their views. There were no pictures in the report so we decided to take some photos.

Show how **one** secondary source helped create knowledge and understanding of an issue. Here, the source also led to decisions about specific primary research.

Now try this

Explain **two** reasons why you chose **one** secondary source in your citizenship action. **(4)**

Only give two reasons. Explain and develop each reason.

Primary research questions

Stage 2 of your citizenship action requires you to carry out primary research to answer research questions and analyse the evidence to assist with decisions on your action. Make sure you can explain how you decided and sequenced your research questions, and your choice of methods.

Primary research

Primary research for your citizenship action involves **two** key things:

1. Discovering new information using your own original research investigations rather than information already published.

2. Identifying what further information you need to research as a result of your secondary research findings.

Research methods

Quantitative methods establish evidence that is **factual** rather than opinion based. It answers questions such as: 'how many' or 'how much'.

Qualitative methods establish evidence about what people **think or feel**. It needs to be interpreted carefully to avoid bias and keep a balanced view.

Choosing methods

The choice of method will reflect what you need to find out. For example, you could carry out

- **interviews** – with people who are directly affected by or involved in your issue
- **focus groups** – small group meetings with key people to establish information
- **surveys** – in person or online using questions to gather views and opinions
- **questionnaires** – with a choice of answers to research a large sample of people
- **asking key targeted questions** – simpler and less numerous than questionnaires
- **physical observation** – related to an area or group you are interested in.

Identifying research questions and actions

Use clear, straightforward questions. Don't have too many or you may lose focus. For example, the questions and actions for reducing congestion near a school (page 115) might be:

Research questions	Research actions
What are the causes of congestion?	Make an observational site visit.
How many vehicles are involved?	Count vehicles on site at different times.
What are the views of the citizens involved?	Interview local residents and road users.
What are the views of local services?	Survey the police and local council.
What are the views of the school?	Interview school management.
Key questions to ask respondents: 1 How far do you agree with the problems identified? 2 Do you think that congestion is so bad that something should be done about it?	Produce and distribute a questionnaire.

Now try this

Write out **two** of your team's key research questions and explain why you thought they were important for your own citizenship action. **(4)**

Your answer must relate specifically to your own citizenship action.

Primary research

For your citizenship action you must explain the primary research methods you chose to answer research questions and show how they provided data for your action. The data then needs to be analysed (see page 118).

Data from primary research

Primary research produces new data which can be obtained in various ways. For example:

- facts and figures from observation
- records of discussions
- qualitative and quantitative interview data
- results of polls, votes and surveys
- visual photographic evidence.

Make sure you meet health and safety and data protection requirements as you research.

Observation

Observation is an excellent way to research a project seeking to influence behaviour. It can produce quantitative data that is expressed numerically, and can use photographs.

For example, the congestion action (page 115) could involve observing:

- vehicles parked in and using the road
- blockages caused by vehicles
- arguments between road users.

Surveys

Surveys can be used online or with small groups or individuals and provide both qualitative and quantitative data. **Polls** are simple one-question surveys. Surveys are useful for awareness raising actions.

For example, the action on criminal and civil law (page 115) could use a survey to:

- establish a group's knowledge and understanding before the activity
- shape the presentation to meet needs
- measure success by repeating the survey at the end of the activity.

Interviews

Interviews are suitable for any citizenship action, including raising awareness. They are time consuming but can produce considerable qualitative and quantitative data. Ask all respondents the same questions.

For example, the action raising awareness about disturbances caused to local residents at home time (page 115) could:

- include interviews with residents, young people and the police
- establish the nature of the disturbance, people's feelings, and resolution so far.

Questionnaires

Questionnaires can be used with large numbers of respondents (people who respond).

- They can provide **quantitative** data usually established by **closed** questions that require 'yes/no' or graded responses, from 'strongly agree' to 'strongly disagree'.
- They can provide **qualitative** data usually established by **open** questions that invite explanations of the respondent's feelings, such as, 'Tell me how you feel about...'

For example, the action on the mock election (page 115) could use a questionnaire to establish issues of interest that could shape election manifestos.

Now try this

Identify **two** different methods of primary research you used in your citizenship action. Choose **one** of them and explain how you used it. **(4)**

Be careful that you do not identify secondary research or a non-research action.

Analysing primary research

For your citizenship action you need to analyse the answers given to your primary research questions and identify evidence that helps your team to refine your action. Make sure you can explain your analysis of **qualitative** and **quantitative** evidence, and your conclusions.

Aims

When you complete primary research, you discover information and evidence to shape and focus your citizenship action.

- Make sure it is as complete as possible. There are few situations which present a single viewpoint so it should both support and challenge your proposed action.

- You may collect a lot of data but the quality will vary. Some will be very useful but some may be unreliable or irrelevant.

- The process of completing, sorting and analysing the data may raise further questions or persuade you to modify your action.

Further questions

Here are **six** key questions to help you understand and shape research evidence.

1. What different points of view are represented?

2. What gaps in your knowledge are revealed?

3. What other questions are raised that require answers?

4. Is qualitative and quantitative data found and are they consistent?

5. Is any evidence irrelevant or unreliable?

6. How does the data justify your proposed action?

Qualitative evidence

Some evidence is qualitative and includes opinion. When put together, you see what it shows. For example, with the congestion action (page 115):

- Most residents might want something done, but disagree on what it should be.

- Some responses will contain facts (can be proved to be true) but most will mainly contain opinion (someone's viewpoint). Sometimes opinion is expressed as if it is fact.

- Some opinions are more helpful than others. Some may see the full picture and others only their own problems.

Quantitative evidence

Some data is quantitative and you need to analyse responses to see what it shows you

For example, with the criminal and civil law action (page 115):

- A survey could establish respondents' knowledge about civil and criminal law by counting how many got each question right or wrong.

- The figures could establish areas to focus on in a presentation.

- Two key question you should ask are:

  1) What does the data show?

  2) Does it provide conclusive answers?

Reaching a conclusion

When analysing evidence, consider how to present your findings and confirm your action.

- Sometimes data can be presented in a list, chart, table or diagram.

- Weigh up all the evidence to see what conclusion it suggests.

- If needed, adjust your action. Identify the steps required to achieve your action.

- Allocate jobs and roles to team members. Make the best use of everyone's skills.

Now try this

Explain the difference between primary and secondary research in your citizenship action.   (2)

Show that you understand both terms and each type of research.

Representing viewpoints

Stage 3 of your citizenship action requires you to represent your own and different points of view. Make sure you can explain how you understood the issue from different perspectives, reviewed evidence, identified the most compelling, and used your findings to decide on actions.

Team viewpoints

Your team should work together to understand and represent different opinions, views and perspectives in relation to your action.

- Groups of friends who work together often think the same way and share interests. They may find it difficult to accommodate different ideas.
- Work with and respect people who hold different viewpoints, not just those you agree with. This will make teamwork more effective.
- Have a wide view, not narrow opinions.
- Consider what is important and think things through properly.

Valuing team members

Make sure your team holds discussions and collaborates when considering different opinions and taking democratic decisions.

- Encourage everyone to contribute ideas and feel respected.
- Listen carefully to what is said, showing that you respect and value different ideas.
- Discuss all suggestions to weigh up which are useful and which are not so useful.
- Justify suggestions and be careful of people's feelings if you reject ideas.

Different viewpoints in research

People often see the same issue in different ways. Your team should decide which evidence is most important.

For example, with the congestion action (page 115):

- A parent collecting a child may think it is unimportant.
- A resident may see it as a major problem.
- The police and other authorities may see it as a legal issue.
- Delivery drivers may think it interferes with them doing their job.
- Teachers and students may think it doesn't concern them.

Understanding relevance

You have to decide what evidence is:

- relevant to your plan and what is not
- compelling and persuasive and what is not
- soundly based and what lacks support or justification.

Most evidence comes from individuals with different identities, personalities, ages and experiences. Different and relevant viewpoints should influence how you develop your action.

Now try this

Explain **two** ways in which your team tried to prevent any disagreements that could lead to arguments or conflict in your citizenship action. **(4)**

Don't describe a difference but show what you did to stop it getting out of hand.

Reviewing viewpoints

For your citizenship action you need to review the research undertaken and the evidence and different viewpoints expressed. Consider why some may be more compelling or persuasive than others, and make the case for what the team think should happen. Make sure you can explain why or how considering different viewpoints helped to improve your citizenship action.

Compelling, persuasive viewpoints	Unconvincing viewpoints
👍 Physical evidence (photos, factual recordings)	👎 Intolerant verbal evidence
👍 Opinions supported with evidence	👎 Assertive but unsupported opinions
👍 Opinions repeated by different respondents	👎 Opinions expressed by only one individual
👍 Relevant evidence and opinions	👎 Irrelevant, lacking involvement with issue
👍 Opinions showing different viewpoints	👎 Biased, unable to consider other viewpoints
👍 Opinions not distorted by passion or anger	👎 Unreliable, inconsistent and inconclusive

Reviewing the evidence and making a case

Making a case for a viewpoint is an opportunity for **advocacy**. Each team member can put forward the action that in their view should move forward, based on the review of evidence.

Judge each case fairly and critically but not negatively. Plans which do not address the below criteria are not suitable and should be modified. Ask if the proposed action could:

- make a difference and have social benefit
- inform, influence and persuade
- raise awareness and understanding
- encourage commitment and activity
- produce a measurable outcome
- let the team meet all six action stages (see page 113).

Ground rules for a review

- Keep written records of discussions
- Set a time limit for each person to make a case
- Give everyone a fair hearing
- Present evidence for the pros and cons
- Set a time limit for questions and discussion
- Do not show disapproval

Confirming the final action

The final choice of action should:

- be **one** of the two types of action outlined on page 113
- be SMART: specific, measurable, achievable, realistic, timebound
- involve everybody and be suited to the skills, resources and time available.

Now try this

Explain how your team decided which of two different viewpoints to accept when proposing your citizenship action plan.   (4)

You need to give the two viewpoints as well as explaining how you chose one of them.

Planning the action

Stage 4 of your citizenship action requires you to plan your action. Make sure you can explain who was the target of the action, the goals and criteria you set for judging success, the plan of action you formed, the roles you allocated, and your system for recording your actions.

Identifying action

Your citizenship action will influence other people. You need to know who to talk to, what you want to achieve, and how to measure the success of your action in:

- raising awareness of an issue
- promoting a response and commitment
- organising an event *or* social action.

Identifying who to target

The desired outcomes of your citizenship action help to identify the target for the action. Investigate who can make things happen. It may be:

- an individual or a group of people
- members of your class, other students, parents, teachers or school governors
- the local council, media or government.

Examples of identifying targets

Here are some target audiences for the examples of citizenship action on page 115.

Example citizenship action	Example target
Raise student awareness of disturbance caused to local residents by students at home time. (Theme A5)	Students Local residents
Organise a mock election to raise awareness among students of the nature of parliamentary elections. (Theme B2)	Students Staff (to get permission for action)
Raise student awareness of differences between civil and criminal law. (Theme C3)	Students Staff (to get permission for action)
Petition the council to reduce problems of congestion near the school. (Theme D1)	Local councillor/council official

Setting goals

You must have SMART goals (specific, measurable, achievable, realistic and timebound). You and your audience should know what you want to achieve and how it will make a difference.

For example, the main goals of three example actions are to raise student awareness. These may persuade students to become interested and active in politics. Goals may also target change in behaviour. For example, in the action related to Theme A, students may become more considerate and tolerant of others and improve the quality of life for residents.

Setting success criteria

As part of your citizenship action you need to set your own success criteria against which you can measure your outcomes. Do not set too many. Make sure they are realistic.

For example, for the action on civil and criminal law, criteria might include: delivering a presentation to students, producing an information leaflet, involving all members of the team, meeting deadlines you have set, testing student knowledge before and after, and showing an improvement in knowledge.

Now try this

Explain **one** of the goals you set for your citizenship action. **(2)**

Your answer must clearly relate to your own citizenship action and not be a general answer that could apply to any action.

Planning tasks and roles

You need to form a clear plan for your citizenship action. Make sure you can explain the methods and approaches you used and how you allocated roles and tasks, kept records, and anticipated difficulties and how to overcome them.

Planning and sequencing action

The method and approach used for planning could divide into **five** parts, for example:

1 As a team, discuss and jot down key tasks.

2 Break down each task into the smaller steps needed to achieve it, including resources.

3 Anticipate difficulties and work out how to overcome them.

4 Make a sequenced list in priority order.

5 Use a table or chart to manage the action plan.

Allocating roles

Your team needs a team leader and people whose jobs include:

- checking that things are done on time
- liaising with your teacher and others
- organising regular team meetings
- acquiring and looking after resources
- keeping brief but accurate records
- ensuring regular communication, which is essential for good teamwork.

Allocating tasks

Match roles and tasks to the skills of each team member so everyone knows:

- exactly what to do
- when the work is to be completed
- whether to work alone or in pairs
- how to present their work to the team
- what to do if they encounter problems
- to report back if the work can't be completed.

Allocating time

Construct a timeline to set a fixed completion date and make the best use of the time available.

- Check the timeline regularly to keep on track, and be prepared to adjust it.
- Allow time for unexpected events so that you can still meet the date.
- Discuss anything that is not working and be prepared to change plans if needed.

Date	Task	Responsibility	Who to see	Completion date	Date completed	Comments

Record-keeping

Brief record-keeping is essential and will help your analysis of how you achieved your goals in the task. Notes should include:

- decisions made and actions agreed
- people met
- resources acquired, including advance room bookings, equipment and training
- data protection and health and safety requirements
- progress made
- difficulties encountered and overcome.

Now try this

Explain **two** ways in which you allocated roles to your team. **(4)**

Do not just say what the roles were. You need to explain the process you used to allocate the roles.

Applying skills in action

Stage 5 of your citizenship action requires you to apply skills of collaboration, negotiation and influencing others as you deliver the action. Make sure you can explain how you demonstrated team work and role awareness in organising and carrying out your action.

Team work and role awareness

Your team will use different skills and roles in **either** organising an event **or** delivering a social action (see page 113). Combining different skills increases a team's strength. Recognising and respecting different roles and skills leads to cooperation and achievement.

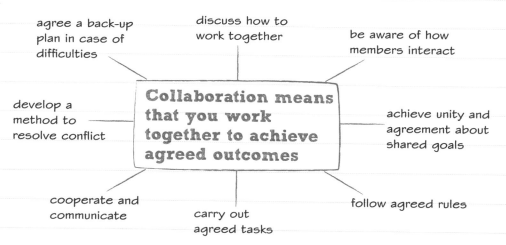

agree a back-up plan in case of difficulties

discuss how to work together

be aware of how members interact

develop a method to resolve conflict

Collaboration means that you work together to achieve agreed outcomes

achieve unity and agreement about shared goals

cooperate and communicate

carry out agreed tasks

follow agreed rules

Negotiation

You may have to negotiate with people of influence and authority. **Negotiation** is discussion designed to reach agreement. Make sure you can explain how successful your negotiations were. Presenting your case effectively may involve:

- recognising that busy people can't waste time
- listening as well as talking
- thinking out and presenting your ideas
- being precise, concise and accurate
- knowing what you want to achieve
- compromising on minor things to get what you want.

Influencing others

You influence people by persuading them to agree with you. Make sure you can explain how you tried to influence others and what methods you used. For example:

- working out the best approach
- seeing things from their perspective
- looking for common ground
- responding positively to different views
- attracting and keeping attention
- anticipating and responding to questions
- dealing with different viewpoints
- using appropriate media.

Presentation skills

Before you make your presentation, test and rehearse your material. Remember **six** key points:

1. Make your key points clearly.
2. Support your arguments with strong evidence.
3. Show passion and commitment.
4. Demonstrate careful and thoughtful plans.
5. Make it easy for your audience to agree with you.
6. Have a short, snappy conclusion.

Now try this

Explain **two** ways that your team demonstrated collaboration in your citizenship action.   (4)

Carrying out the action

You should demonstrate skills appropriate to the citizenship action you carry out. Make sure you can explain what skills your action demonstrated, and the methods you used.

contribute to TV or radio phone-ins

correspond with influential people

hold a meeting and make a presentation

use open air drama for publicity

print copies of correspondence in letter pages of newspapers

publicise your analysis of questionnaires and surveys

use questionnaires and surveys

Skills and methods might include:

hold demonstrations or public protests

produce leaflets, posters, banners, placards

set up a website or use social media

arrange a display in your local library or meeting place

use photos of appropriate locations, people or objects

lobby councillors, MPs or other influential people

involve the local media

use emails or distribute newsletters

Organising an event – an example

For an event to raise student awareness of differences between civil and criminal law (see page 114) you might arrange a meeting of fellow students. You may have to:

1   Book a room and a time
2   Advertise your activity
3   Get the approval of your teachers
4   Present the findings of your initial survey
5   Identify areas of weak knowledge
6   Present information about the law
7   Use visual aids to support the explanation
8   Have a question and answer session
9   Repeat the survey with the audience
10 Present the outcome
11 Assess the level of success achieved
12 Identify improvements in knowledge

Organising social action – an example

For an event such as reducing congestion near the school (see page 114) you might arrange a petition. You may have to:

Share tasks between team members to show involvement, negotiation, collaboration and influence.

1   Survey local residents about congestion
2   Produce photographic evidence
3   Compile results of a survey
4   Publicise with display in school or locally
5   Arrange meeting(s) with local councillors
6   Contact local newspapers/radio/TV
7   Raise concerns in discussion with police
8   Publicise with public demo and placards
9   Spark debate in letters page of local press
10 Draw up petition and collect signatures
11 Give petition to councillors (with media)
12 Submit report and photos to local media
13 Attend council meetings
14 Circulate a newsletter

Now try this

Explain **one** of the methods you used to achieve your goals when you carried out your citizenship action and say whether you would do it in the same way again.

(4)

Evaluating the action

Stage 6 requires you to critically evaluate your learning and the impact of your citizenship action. A useful way to evaluate is to measure your work using a series of questions.

Assessing your action against your goals

Consider how and why your action did, or did not, achieve its intended effect. Assess the success of your activity in relation to your goals and success criteria (page 122).

1. Can you say how your action affected behaviour, made people more aware, or helped change the social environment?

2. How were you able to persuade people in positions of authority and influence to accept or support your proposals?

3. What evidence do you have to show that your action influenced others?

Assessing your methods

Assess how well your selected methods worked in practice and what you might do differently in a future action.

1. Did you choose appropriate methods to achieve your goals?

2. Did any of your selected methods interfere with your progress?

3. Can you show that all team members were actively involved throughout?

Assessing the impact on learning

Consider the impact of your citizenship action on your learning, including mistakes.

1. Would you set different goals if you were to repeat the activity?

2. What problems or difficulties did team work create?

3. Was the outcome a compromise between what you wanted to do and what you could actually do?

Assessing your own role

Here are **seven** questions to help you assess and explain the part you played in your citizenship action and how it affected you.

1. What was your role in the team?

2. What did you do well?

3. What could you have done differently or more successfully?

4. How did you react to different ideas and viewpoints?

5. How have your communication skills improved?

6. How has your citizenship action confirmed or changed your opinions?

7. Are you more or less committed now than when you started the action?

Citizenship action can make a powerful impact. What advice would you give to others starting citizenship action?

Now try this

'Good communication between team members is just as important as the methods they use when carrying out a citizenship action.' How far do you agree with this view? You must base your answer on your experience of your own citizenship action. Give reasons for your opinion showing that you have considered another point of view.　**(12)**

Your answer must refer to your own experiences in carrying out your citizenship action, and show the part played by good communication and the methods you used.

Section A questions

In **Section A, Own citizenship action**, there is one question that is divided into parts, and focuses on **Theme E: Taking citizenship action**. Base your answers on the knowledge and understanding you gained with **your own citizenship action**.

Paper 2 Section A Own citizenship action

At the beginning of Section A, you will be asked to write the title of your citizenship action in no more than 20 words. You need to indicate what the action is about, the nature of the action to be taken, who is to be affected, and demonstrate a clear link with a specific part of a chosen theme. Here are some examples, one for each theme.

Worked example

Own citizenship action
You have been part of a group that organised and took part in a citizenship action. In no more than 20 words, write the title of your citizenship action below.

Theme A example:
Petitioning a shop owner to lift their ban on groups of teenagers being in the shop. (A3)

This is based on Theme A3, 'Encouraging mutual understanding'. It is a social action about justice and equality. It is achievable and can bring about change.

Theme B example:
Raising student awareness of arguments supporting the extension of voting rights to 16-year-olds. (B2)

This is based on Theme B2, 'Who can and cannot vote'. It is about raising awareness and involves power and justice. It is manageable and can influence views.

Theme C example:
Campaigning to secure student membership of a school committee that reviews school rules. (C1)

This is based on Theme C3, 'How the law affects our daily lives'. It is a social action about participation and democracy. It is realistic and could lead to change.

Theme D example:
Raising parental awareness of proposals to sell the school playing fields for housing. (D2)

This is based on Theme D2, 'Actions to address public policy'. It is an awareness-raising action and is about accountability, power and justice. It is practicable and could lead to further action.

Now try this

Explain **two** reasons behind your choice of citizenship action title. **(4)**

For each reason, give the reason and then develop the explanation each time.

Short answer questions

Paper 2, Section A, focuses on **Theme E: Taking citizenship action**. Questions requiring short answers are based on your knowledge and understanding of citizenship concepts, terms and issues applied to your own citizenship action. Here are some examples.

Worked example

Explain **one** problem you experienced when working as a member of a team in your citizenship action. **(2)**

Everybody wanted to talk at the same time about our petition. This was difficult because we didn't know what people were saying, and some of them started to shout to be heard. It only stopped when Sam took charge and tried to control them.

Explain **one** method you used when carrying out primary research in your citizenship action. **(2)**

We conducted a survey of students in our class. We did this to find out how many of them believed that 16-year-olds should have the right to vote.

After completing your research, you will have analysed your findings. Explain **one** finding which was useful and **one** which was irrelevant. **(4)**

Useful. We did a survey which showed that most parents did not know about the proposal to sell the school fields. It was useful because it showed us that our action to raise awareness did have a useful purpose.

Irrelevant. In our survey one parent said she never enjoyed PE at school and so didn't think the fields were needed. We ignored this because no one else said this, and we thought it was irrelevant because the project wasn't about not liking sport but about having the opportunity to do it.

For 'explain' questions you should make a point or give an example, then develop your answer to show your understanding. Answers must be clearly linked to your citizenship action.

This answer relates to Theme A and is clearly based on personal experience. It states the problem and then develops it to explain why it was a problem.

Read questions carefully. Your chosen method must relate to **primary** (not secondary) research. State the method and then explain how or why you used it. This answer relates to Theme B and clearly names the method (survey) and develops the answer by explaining why the method was chosen.

Make sure that for **each** finding you give an example, and then develop your answer to demonstrate understanding, applied to your citizenship action.

This answer relates to Theme D. It makes a point for **each** finding and goes on to develop it.

The reason the finding was irrelevant is clearly given and illustrates how participation and democracy work within citizenship action.

Now try this

Explain **one** reason why **either** qualitative **or** quantitative evidence was useful when planning your citizenship action. **(2)**

Choose **either** qualitative **or** quantitative evidence to explain. Show you understand what it means and how you used it.

Long answer question

In **Paper 2, Section A**, one question requires a longer answer based on **your citizenship action.** You should:

- show knowledge about the concepts, terms and issues in relation to your citizenship action and contexts
- make a convincing and sustained analysis of viewpoints
- give reasoned and coherent arguments in your evaluation, showing breadth and depth
- come to a conclusion with an overall judgement that is substantiated by your evidence.

Worked example

'Secondary research is more important than primary research when embarking on a citizenship action.' How far do you agree with this view?

You **must** base your answer on your experience of **your own** citizenship action.

Give reasons for your opinion, showing that you have considered another point of view. **(12)**

Consider how this answer:

- relates clearly to your own action.
- considers another point of view.
- relates to the example of citizenship action for Theme B on page 127 and shows knowledge.

Secondary research uses existing data to build a general background. Primary research is collected as part of the citizenship action and finds brand new information specific to the action. Both are vital to completing a successful citizenship action.

In relation to reducing voting age, secondary research shows the current position on voting age and arguments for and against, such as lack of maturity, or the fact that those aged 16 can do other things that need maturity, such as join the army with parental consent. As part of the Scottish independence referendum, those aged 16 were allowed to vote as the decision affected their future. This justified their involvement. All this secondary research provided a base for the rest of the citizenship action, so used time effectively.

Primary research allowed us to find out feelings about the issue from various groups such as parents, other adults and those aged 16 themselves. This kind of information can change a lot, so completing primary research gave us an up-to-date range of evidence. This qualitative evidence from interviews showed support for lowering the voting age, giving a good indication of people's current views. Some older people, however, felt that 16-year-olds were not mature enough.

Secondary research has another use as it identified two local councillors who did not support the change to voting age, so we were able to target them to try to persuade them to change to our point of view.

Secondary research is more important because it gives a factual base for primary research, identifies who to talk to and suggests different arguments to explore. Without this we might not have been clear about primary research, and what to try and achieve from it.

Now try this

Consider how far you agree with the view that: 'Team members who disagree about their citizenship action should stop arguing and accept the majority view.' Make notes of key points to answer this question, based on your own experience of citizenship action. Give reasons for your opinion, showing you have considered another point of view.

Practice short answer questions

Practise for **Paper 2, Section A, Own citizenship action** with these exam-style short answer questions. Example answers are provided (page 132 forward)

Guided

You have been part of a group that organised and took part in a citizenship action. In no more than 20 words, write the title of your citizenship action below.

....

....

....

> You must give the title of your own citizenship action. See page 126 for examples.

Explain **one** reason why it may be better in a citizenship action for a team to consist of more than just close friends. **(2)**

....

....

....

> Make sure you link your answer to your own citizenship action.

Explain **one** way in which working in pairs might be sensible when doing primary research for your citizenship action. **(2)**

....

....

....

> Give **one** way, then develop your point. Your answer should be about participation.

Explain **two** of the criteria your team set for judging the success of your citizenship action. **(4)**

1 ....

....

....

2 ....

....

....

> The question is not about whether you succeeded or not, but about what measures you agreed by which to judge the action and its outcome.

Your citizenship action will have involved negotiation with others. This may have been a person of authority or in a position of influence. Explain one way in which this was helpful and one way in which it proved difficult. **(4)**

One way in which this was helpful:

....

....

....

> This may be a teacher or official who helped your action, or whom you need to persuade.

One way in which this was difficult:

....

....

....

> Explain how it helped to progress your activity.

> Then explain what the difficulty was and whether you could use your communication skills.

Practice long answers

Practise for **Paper 2, Section A, Own citizenship action** with this exam-style long answer question that requires extended writing. Example answers are provided (page 132 forward).

Guided

'In a citizenship action it is better for one person to allocate tasks and roles to team members than to let each of them volunteer for what they want to do.'

How far do you agree with this view?

You must base your answer on your experience of your own citizenship action.

Give reasons for your opinion, showing that you have considered another point of view.

(12)

....
....
....
....
....
....
....
....
....
....
....
....
....
....
....
....
....
....
....
....
....
....

This is about your **own** citizenship action. Make your action clear at the start of your answer to set your views in context. Your answer could address issues of democracy, equality and participation.

Consider the following in your answer:

- **Your** knowledge and understanding as applied to your citizenship action.
- More viewpoints than just your own.
- Your evaluation of your action and the interaction of the group. Make sure this links back to the focus of the question.
- Presenting a coherent argument supported with evidence from your own experience.
- A conclusion supported by your evidence and examples.

Continue your answer on a separate piece of paper.

Answers

Theme A: Living together in the UK

1 The changing UK population

Individual responses. For example: The UK has an increasingly ageing population, which impacts on government spending. For example, age-related conditions such as dementia place increasing demand on funding for NHS treatment or for social and personal care.

2 Migration and its impact

Individual responses. For example: Compliance with the Human Rights Act 1998.

3 Sources of migration

D Latvia. Latvia is a member of the EU and is not a member of the Commonwealth.

4 Mutual respect

Individual responses. For example: One way that mutual respect is upheld is through laws such as The Equality Act 2010. The Equality Act protects people from discrimination such as sexism, racism, ageism and homophobia.

5 Mutual understanding

Individual responses. For example: Through education. For example, teaching Citizenship or Religious Education informs students about different cultures, traditions and religions and develops greater understanding.

6 Defining identify

Individual responses. For example:
1. Age can change individual identity. For example, an individual might identify with travelling and extreme sports when younger. This may change as the person gets older, especially if they take on the responsibilities of a parent.
2. Gender can change individual identity. For example, an individual born in one gender might choose to change to another gender, with changes in appearance, clothing, and practical aspects such as which public toilets they use.

7 Identity debates

Individual responses. For example:
1. Religious factors may be important to a person's identity. For example, a person from Northern Ireland may identify with Protestant religious beliefs which also helped shape their history.
2. Geographic factors may also be important. For example, a person living in London may identify their nationality as British rather than English, as they are closer to political and royal events in the capital city that often represent Britain as a whole.

8 Human and moral rights

Individual responses. For example:
1. Prisoners sentenced and held in British prisons are denied the right to vote. However, the European Convention on Human Rights states that everyone can vote, even if they are in prison.
2. Some feel that homeless people are denied the right to a basic standard of living. This is a human right in the Universal Declaration of Human Rights.

9 Legal rights

Individual responses. For example:
Consumers purchasing goods or services are protected by The Consumer Rights Act 2015. For example, if the good or service is not as advertised, they have a right to make an exchange, claim money back, or for a repeat service to be carried out properly.

10 Political rights

Two of the following: general elections; local council elections; referendums; mayoral elections; Police and Crime Commissioner elections.

11 The rule of law

One of the following, for example: access to justice; equality before the law; innocent until proven guilty.

12 Magna Carta and developing rights

Two of the following, for example: the right to a fair trial; access to justice; trial by jury of peers; nobody is above the law.

13 Protecting rights and freedoms

The correct answer is C: The Human Rights Act 1998.

14 Protecting human rights

Individual responses. For example:
1. The right to participate in politics, for example voting in an election or standing for election.
2. The right to freedom of peaceful assembly or association, for example arranging a march or rally as a pressure group protest.

15 Citizens and local government

Individual responses. For example:
1. Social housing, often called council housing. This typically provides low-income families with affordable rented accommodation.
2. Different kinds of leisure services. Examples of these include skate parks, paddling pools, carnivals and firework displays.

16 Paying for local services

Individual responses. For example: Local government funding is boosted by local business rates. By encouraging new business and enterprise they are increasing their income.

Paper 1 Section A: Living together in the UK

17 Short answer questions

The Equality Act 2010.

18 Source A questions 1

Individual responses. For example: One similarity is that they are both ageing. One difference is that although the countries are the same size, the UK population is 12 times larger.

19 Source A questions 2

Individual responses. For example:
1. With an ageing population there are fewer people of working age. This means there is less money being paid in tax to pay for pensions and care, so taxes may have to go up.
2. Older people may suffer illnesses and physical disabilities. This puts an increasing burden on health services which may already be overstretched and can't pay for all the treatment needed.

20 Practice short answer questions

Multiple choice question: the correct answer is C, to be treated fairly and without discrimination. This is confirmed in the Human Rights Act 1998.

For the incorrect answers: A is an entitlement under English law (within limits), but is not a human right. The human right is the 'right to education'. B is not correct. Under English law a person may use 'reasonable force' to protect property. It is not a human right. **D** is a right provided under English law but it is not a human right as defined in the Human Rights Act 1998.

Give question: Individual responses. For example, **one** of: increased tax payments; addresses skill shortages; creates more culturally diverse communities.

Suggest question: Individual responses. For example:
1. Some of the council's income comes from central government. This amount has been steadily reduced in recent years.
2. Some money comes from business rates. This amount may have reduced because large numbers of shops have closed down and no longer pay it.

Other reasons might include: government cap on how much council tax can be increased; council tax bands are out of date and need to be revised; effects of inflation; rising cost of essential/statutory services.

Explain question (mayors): Individual responses. For example: Traditional mayors are elected by the councillors but the general public choose elected mayors. This means elected mayors have a mandate for the work they do.

Other answers could refer to: period of office (directly elected mayors serve for four-year periods, but traditional mayors are usually chosen by the council for a single year); ceremonial or executive (directly elected mayors have an executive role to determine policy and spending plans in their authority, but traditional mayors have a ceremonial role as a figurehead for the council); control of budget (directly elected mayors are in overall control of a council's spending, but traditional mayors are not); policy making (directly elected mayors are political appointments and have a mandate based on the policies they propose, but traditional mayors do not control policy unless they are also the leader of the council).

Explain question (respect): Individual responses. For example:
1. We live in a diverse society made up of people with different backgrounds and interests. Respect is therefore needed to make sure that communities can get along and are productive together.
2. Equality laws and the Human Rights Act 1998 say we should show respect to other people. If we don't show respect we could encourage conflict and violence and break the law.

21 Practice Source A questions

Individual responses using the source and adding your own knowledge to what you learn from the source. This might include some of the points below, for example.
- It is wrong to place blame entirely on central government or on local government for this financial crisis. The picture suggests that councils lack money to carry out basic work. Successive governments have imposed cuts on grants to local government and have limited the permitted level of council tax and business rates rises. In 2010, the Local Government Minister, Eric Pickles, was one of the first department heads to accept cuts. He accepted a cut of 27%.
- The Tory party clearly believed then (and now) that most councils were inefficient and wasteful, and that savings could easily be made by reducing unnecessary spending. This point by a minister is given in the source in relation to Tory councils in difficulties.
- It is also true that in recent years, government has added to the statutory responsibilities of councils, in particular relating to children's services and care of the elderly. Some claim that austerity has carried on for too long and is now causing damage, rather than improving efficiency and ending waste. The potholes are a good example of this.
- The implication is that Tories feel local government needs to be reduced in size and restricted to a limited range of services.
- On the other hand, councils can be wasteful and extravagant. There are references in the source to high salaries paid to chief executives, and grants made to minority groups and cultural

activities. These suggest a need for more careful targeting of limited funds. Some councils are better able to balance their budgets. These are mainly wealthy Tory councils. Councils in deprived areas are likely to overspend because extra services are needed.
- Salaries are a major cost. Pay rates are often controlled centrally (there has been a 1% cap for many years). Senior positions are recruited from the private sector so there is a need to compete with salaries offered in the private sector. Some factors are outside central or local government control. For example, effects of inflation; ageing population requiring increased spending; rising cost of services which are outstripping income; EU directives; low interest rates on investments/reserves but high interest rates on borrowing.
- Councils have to set priorities with limited funds. Spending in one area is at the cost of not spending in another area. For example, the need to support social care means reduced spending on leisure, culture and roads.
- The funding crisis is caused by several factors including reduced income and increasing costs. Both central and local government have to accept some responsibility. The real problem is the scope of work expected of local government. The caption shows that the cost of the crisis is being born by the general public. There is a need to rethink the roles and responsibilities of local government.

Theme B: Democracy at work in the UK

22 Major political parties

Individual responses. For example:
1. Liberal Democrats believe in reinstating grants for the poorest university students.
2. Conservatives believe in improving perceived school standards, e.g. by creating more selective (e.g. grammar) schools.

23 How candidates are selected

Individual responses. For example, **two** of the following: aged over 18; a British citizen; an Irish citizen; a qualifying Commonwealth citizen; have a £500 deposit; have the backing of 10 of the electorate; authorised to stand for a political party OR choosing to be an independent candidate.

24 The concept of democracy

Individual responses. For example:
1. Elections only take place every five years. This means that citizens don't have much say in the work of government between elections.
2. MPs usually vote in support of their party. As a result, they don't always represent the views of their constituency.

25 General elections

Individual responses. For example:
1. One reason argued is that 16-year-olds are too immature to vote. They could easily be influenced by peers or family members.
2. Another reason argued is that 16-year-olds do not know enough about politics to make an informed decision. They may be unlikely to research the different party manifestos to find out what each party is promising.

26 Voting systems

Individual responses. For example:
1. Candidates can be elected on little public support, as a candidate needs to get the most votes, not a majority of votes. Therefore, the majority of a constituency might have voted for other candidates.

2. Votes can be wasted. If a voter lives in a safe seat but prefers a different candidate or party then it is likely their vote will not have an effect on the election or give them any representation.

27 Forming a government

Individual responses. For example:
1. With a majority government it is easier to pass laws. A government with a majority of MPs to support their policies makes it harder for the opposition to stop laws being created.
2. It means that parties do not have to compromise their policies. If a party is in a coalition then they may have to compromise their policies to work with a different party that has a different ideology.

28 Organisation of a government

Individual responses. For example:
1. To advise government ministers. This may be on the policy they wish to implement, and any problems there may be.
2. To impartially serve any government that may be elected. This means that senior civil servants have to be politically neutral.

29 Westminster Parliament

Individual responses. For example:
1. To interpret the laws created by Parliament and, if no jury is present, decide the verdict.
2. To decide on sentencing. This is based upon recommended sentences usually provided by Parliament as part of the law that they have passed.

30 Houses of Commons and Lords

Individual responses. For example:
1. Proposing new law. Often the government will put forward new laws promised as part of their manifesto.
2. Scrutinising wider areas of government policy. This may be completed by a select committee.

31 The roles of ministers and MPs

Individual responses. For example:
1. To keep order in the House of Commons. This can be done by suspending the House where necessary.
2. To chair debates. This can be done by the speaker selecting MPs to speak, in order to ensure debate actually happens.

32 Making and shaping law

Individual responses. For example:
1. To act on their election promise to implement all new laws proposed in their manifesto.
2. In response to media or pressure group actions.

33 The British Constitution

Individual responses. For example:
1. To provide an alternative to the current government.
2. To scrutinise the work of government.
3. To suggest amendments to bills proposed by government.

34 Uncodified constitution

Individual responses. For example:
1. UK legislation.
2. Conventions.
3. Common law.

35 Parliamentary sovereignty

Individual responses. For example: In the British constitution, parliamentary sovereignty describes how Parliament is the main law-making body and cannot be overruled. In parliamentary sovereignty, future Parliaments can make their own laws and amend or remove any existing laws.

36 Devolution in the UK

Individual responses. For example:
1. Health.
2. Education.

37 Changing relations

Individual responses. For example: Devolution has given the Welsh the power to legislate. They have introduced laws that strengthen the Welsh identity, such as the requirement to treat the Welsh and English languages equally. This ensures that the historic national identity and language of Wales is not forgotten or ignored.

38 Direct and indirect taxes

Individual responses. For example:
1. Income tax.
2. Inheritance tax.
3. Corporation tax.

39 The Chancellor of the Exchequer

Individual responses. For example: A key responsibility of the Chancellor of the Exchequer is to manage the budget, balancing expenditure against income. For example, the Chancellor might have to cut the education budget in order to reduce expenditure.

40 Budget and provision

Individual responses. For example:
1. Public opinion that the NHS should remain free to all.
2. Demand due to an ageing population.

Paper 1 Section B: Democracy at work in the UK

41 Short answer questions

Individual responses. For example:
1. The job of the House of Lords is to scrutinise bills passed by the House of Commons. Taking a second look reveals problems and allows suggested improvements and revisions to be made.
2. Most members of the House of Lords are appointed. This allows experts from different fields to be involved in the scrutiny, including members of minority groups who might not be represented in Parliament, which makes the scrutiny more effective.

42 Source B questions 1

Individual responses. For example: A 'confidence and supply' agreement is an agreement to support a government on a vote-by-vote basis. Support will usually be given when a party agrees with the government's proposal, or if there is an attempt to defeat it and force an election.

43 Source B questions 2

Individual responses. For example: The Conservatives were in a stronger position than in 2010 because they were only eight votes short, and Sinn Fein don't attend Parliament which meant they really only needed six extra votes. The SNP and Liberal Democrats refused a coalition with the Conservatives. If Teresa May had made a formal coalition, she would have had to make policy concessions, but an informal agreement was less limiting on what she could do.

44 Practice short answer questions

Identify question: Individual responses. For example: To help cover the cost of a rapidly increasing, ageing population.
Explain question: Individual responses. For example:
1. The government (the executive) is separate from and answerable to Parliament (the legislature). This means Parliament can supervise the government and control what it is doing.
2. The judiciary (legal system) is independent of the government and Parliament so it cannot be told what to do.

Multiple choice question (voting, Scottish Assembly): the correct answer is **C**, additional member vote (in combination with first-past-the-post). For the other options: **A** was used in electing MEPs, Northern Ireland Assembly, and local authorities and Scottish local authorities. **B** was used to elect MEPs in the European Parliament. **D** is used to elect directly elected Mayors and Police and Crime Commissioners.

Multiple choice question (general public vote): the correct answer is: **C** The Mayor of Greater Manchester. **A** is a senior civil servant who is appointed and not elected; **B** is the head of the judiciary and appointed by a specially appointed committee; **D** is elected by MPs in the House of Commons.

Name question: Individual responses. For example, **one** of the following: scrutiny, proposing legislation, debate, holding government to account, recruitment of government.

Suggest question: Individual responses. For example, **one** of the following:
- Wales is a smaller country with a smaller population.
- There was less demand for devolution in Wales than in Scotland, resulting in fewer powers.
- Wales has not been a separate country for many centuries and so there is less recent history of independence.

45 Practice Source B questions

Individual responses which might include some of the points below, for example.
- Both countries have two-chamber law-making bodies. In the UK only the House of Commons is elected. The House of Lords is a revising chamber made up of appointed not elected members.
- In Italy both houses of Parliament have to agree an identical text before a bill may become law. In the UK the House of Lords can suggest amendments, but the House of Commons makes the final decision.
- Both countries use committees to revise and propose legislation, but in Italy the main committee work is done before a bill is proposed in Parliament. In the UK a bill is scrutinised and revised by committee after the first reading.
- In Italy, regional parliaments can propose laws for consideration by the national parliament. In the UK, there are three devolved regions (Scotland, Wales and Northern Ireland). All have some law-making powers, but Scotland has much greater power than the other two.
- After discussion in committee, amended bills are reported back to the chamber for further debate and discussion. In both countries the bill is discussed clause by clause and any amendments are voted on.
- When finally agreed the bill is sent in both cases to the other chamber for agreement. In the UK the House of Lords can propose amendments but these have to be considered and either accepted or rejected by the Commons. The final House of Commons version is then sent for royal assent. In Italy both chambers have to agree the final text, and so a bill may be sent backwards and forward several times until agreement is reached on identical wording.
- In Italy, the agreed bill is then sent to the President for approval. He may accept it, in which case it becomes law, or he may send it back to Parliament for further discussion. He has to accept it when Parliament returns it to him. In the UK, royal assent is a ceremonial formality. Unlike the Italian President, the Queen does not have the power or constitutional right to amend or reject a law. In effect the House of Commons is the supreme law-making body.

Theme C: Law and justice

46 The role of law

Individual responses. For example:
1. Society might be very chaotic as people would do what they wanted.

2. There would be no laws against stealing, so people could take things that did not belong to them.
3. Society could become more violent if there was no law against assault or murder.

47 Law in society

Individual responses. For example:
1. To protect people from harm.
2. To help solve disputes between people.
3. To help prevent discrimination against people.

48 Age of legal responsibility

Individual responses. For example: Those aged 16 may be vulnerable to being exploited. For example, an employer might make them work too many hours, which could hurt their education or damage their health if the law did not forbid this.

49 Principles of law

Individual responses. For example: The rule of law is a fundamental principle to uphold citizens' rights and freedoms. It means that no-one is above the law, and all must obey it and be held accountable for their actions, regardless of their position in society, whether a monarch or an ordinary citizen.

50 Regional legal systems

Individual responses. For example: Scotland does not use common law. England and Wales have a common law system, as does Northern Ireland. Scotland is different because it kept its own legal system when it joined the UK in the 18th century. This means it uses Scots law, which is based on Roman law rather than common law.

51 Sources of law

Individual responses. For example: One way is by Parliament making new legislation which becomes statute law. Another way is by judges interpreting existing law to set precedents for other judges to follow.

52 Criminal and civil law

Individual responses. For example: Criminal law maintains order and protects the public from harm. It is concerned with actions that break the criminal law and are against a person (such as murder) or property (such as stealing). It is dealt with in the Magistrates' Court, or more serious cases are heard in the Crown Court.

53 England and Wales justice system 1

Individual responses. For example:
1. To apply the law in all cases they hear.
2. To pass sentence on the guilty.

54 England and Wales justice system 2

Individual responses. For example:
1. To deal with minor cases in criminal law such as criminal damage.
2. To pass sentence on the guilty.

55 Roles of citizens

Individual responses. For example:
1. Volunteering to become a special constable.
2. Serving on a jury.
3. Becoming a magistrate.

56 Law in practice

Individual responses. For example:
1. To ensure the person knows why they are being arrested, which respects their human rights to a fair trial and a fair justice system.
2. To ensure that an arrested person has the right of access to impartial legal advice, so they are protected against unfair treatment.

57 Criminal courts

Individual responses. For example:
Magistrates' Court: a summary offence such as criminal damage.
Crown Court: an indictable offence such as murder.

58 Civil courts

Individual responses. For example:
Payment of debts.

59 Tribunals

Individual responses. For example:
1. Mediation is quicker that going to court.
2. Mediation is cheaper than going to court.

60 Youth justice

Individual responses. For example: Youth courts are more informal than adult courts. Defendants are called by their first name, and the public cannot attend so the defendant's identity is protected.

61 Youth sentencing

Individual responses. For example: One aim of youth courts is to stop young people reoffending. If young people realise the impact of their crime and are involved in a community sentence with education and training, it may turn them away from crime in future.

62 Crime rates

Individual responses. For example:
1. They may lack confidence in the police to tackle the issue. They may avoid getting involved in the justice system if they believe nothing will be done about the crime.
2. Victims may be afraid that the criminal will seek revenge. They worry that the criminal will find a way to harm them or repeat the crime again.

63 Reducing crime

Individual responses. For example: Increasing the number of community police on patrol and visiting schools in a community could be effective to prevent crime. This would build more relationships in the community, and the police presence and education may mean that young people avoid committing crimes.

64 Sentence and punishment

Individual responses. For example:
1. Fines.
2. Community payback.

65 The purpose of punishment

Individual responses. For example: It is a type of punishment where an offender 'pays back' their debt to society. For example, a person found guilty of damaging a neighbour's garden may be given community service working to tidy a local nature reserve.

Paper 1 Section C: Law and justice

66 Short answer questions

Individual responses. For example:
Retributive justice is based on the idea that offenders deserve to suffer punishment in proportion to their offence. The sentence is about punishment and not about rehabilitation.

67 Source C questions 1

Individual responses. For example:
1. They attend youth courts when young offenders are on trial.
2. They supervise young offenders when carrying out community service orders.

68 Source C questions 2

Individual responses. For example:
1. Young people are more likely to be able to change their ways and behaviour. A youth court therefore focuses on rehabilitating offenders to stop them committing crime.

2. Young people can be dealt with more informally than in an adult court. Parents and carers can support the young person, and they remain anonymous so that rehabilitation is more effective.

69 Practice short answer questions

Explain question: Individual responses. For example: Criminal courts deal with breaches of criminal law such as murder and rape, and can give custodial sentences. Civil courts deal with civil cases such as disputes between individuals or groups, and give sentences such as fines rather than custodial sentences.

Suggest question: Any one of: Conditional or absolute discharge, community service, fine, referral to a Youth Offending Team, youth rehabilitation order.

Multiple choice question: the correct answer is **B** 'interpretations of the law made by judges when giving verdicts'.

Give question: Individual responses. For example, one of: get married with parental consent, apply for legal aid, receive a youth rehabilitation order, be detained in custody (but not in an adult centre), leave home without parents/carers permission, apply to the council for their own home, (technically) buy their own home, legally give consent to sex, join the army with parental consent, access their school records.

Identify question: Magistrates' Court.

Explain question: Individual responses. For example:
1. Statute law. Parliament is the main law-making body and is responsible for most new laws.
2. Common law. This is made by judges deciding cases and those decisions being followed in future.

70 Practice Source C questions

Individual responses which might include some of the points below, for example.
- USA has a 'tough on crime' policy that encourages longer prison terms, but the UK seeks to use alternative methods where possible that seek to avoid reoffending, though political parties have sometimes advocated 'tough on crime' policies that include longer sentences.
- Both countries have privatised as well as state-run facilities. In the USA, each state has its own legal system. In the UK, each country operates its own legal and prison system.
- Powers of judges in the USA are increasingly restricted. This includes mandatory sentencing, and the obligation to ignore mitigating circumstances. The UK encourages judges to consider mitigating circumstances and allows sentencing discretion.
- In the USA many states have a 'three strikes and you're out' approach, but the UK uses suspended sentences for first time offenders. The USA imprisons for relatively minor crimes whereas the UK tries to use imprisonment for more serious crimes, or where there is a threat or danger to society. The USA uses imprisonment to protect society but the UK is increasingly attempting rehabilitation.
- The UK has two types of prison sentencing: determinate and indeterminate. Determinate sentencing has a fixed term of which half is served in prison and the rest in the community. Indeterminate sentencing is where there is no fixed length. Sometimes a minimum term is set, with no release until an individual is proven not to pose a threat to society.
- USA has the world's largest prison population (about one-fifth of the world's total of over 10m prisoners for crime, or 655 per 100,000 of the population), while the UK has 80,000, or 146 per 100,000. The USA has had a rapid increase in prison population, but the UK is working to reduce the prison population and use alternative, more effective forms of punishment.

Paper 1 Section D: Citizenship issues and debates

71–72 Source D questions

Individual responses for Emily Thornberry. For example:
1. They should be able to vote on issues that will affect the rest of their lives.

2. Many may have proved their responsibility by caring for members of their family who are elderly or disabled.

Individual responses for David Lidington. For example:

1. Most EU countries think 18 is the right age at which to give people the vote.
2. Labour raised the minimum legal age for some activities so young people were responsible enough and voting is more important so it should stay at 18.

73 Short answer questions

Voting is about making a responsible decision.

75–76 Linked theme questions

Individual responses that might include the following points, for example.

- It is true that local councils are in closer touch with the wishes of their constituents than the government, but it is also true that different areas of the country have different needs. The government is responsible for the economy of the country as a whole, so it is their responsibility to decide what the country can afford and what it needs. The government has the right to set its priorities because that is what they were elected to do.
- We have been told frequently that as a country we are spending far more than we can afford. It is the government's opinion that local authorities are extravagant and wasteful. By cutting the amount of money they give to councils they force the councils to decide what their real priorities are.
- Local councils must work within the resources they have. If this means they have to reduce unnecessary spending then their position is no different to the rest of the population. You can't spend more than you have got and it is right that the government has explained this.

77–78 Practice Source D questions

Multiple choice question ('Yes' viewpoint): the correct answer is **C**, increased tax on the rich would not harm the UK's economic recovery.

Multiple choice question ('No' viewpoint): the correct answer is **D**, tax cuts for the poorest in society have been proved in the past to help economic recovery.

Analyse question. Individual responses. For example:

1. Changes to Corporation Tax do influence the UK's international trading position.
2. Radical tax changes are needed if the UK's economy is to prosper.

Which writer do you agree with more?

Individual responses, that might include some of the following points, for example:

- Jones seems more interested in increasing taxes on the wealthy, whereas Nelson is more concerned with reducing taxes for the poorer sections of population.
- Nelson blames the problems of the economy on the policy of the Bank of England (low interest rates and high government borrowing), but Jones suggests it is because the rich are not paying their fair share.
- Jones wants a radical taxation policy especially on the wealthiest but Nelson wants targeted tax cuts mainly for the poorest.
- Jones supports his view by saying high tax economies (and the UK in the past) prospered in contrast to the economic problems of today associated with lower taxes. Nelson blames policies of government and the Bank of England which have artificially made the wealthy wealthier.
- Jones feels that heavy taxation on the rich will have little effect on their wealth or lifestyle, but Nelson is more concerned with the gap that has developed between rich and poor. Assets of the rich get more valuable but the poor are not able to save or buy houses.
- Jones says nothing about taxes on the poorest, but Nelson argues in favour of tax cuts to help them.

- Jones supports his argument with evidence from opinion polls and surveys showing there is popular support for increasing taxes on the rich. Nelson does not provide this type of supporting evidence for his viewpoint.
- Jones sees taxes on the wealthy and Corporation Tax increases as raising vast sums for the Treasury, but Nelson says nothing about this in his viewpoint.
- Both see Corporation Tax as key to the UK's international trade, but Jones wants to increase it while Nelson wants to reduce it.
- Both agree that the wealthy have benefitted more than the poor from recent economic policy.
- Both recognise the UK is facing an economic challenge which needs to be dealt with. Both agree this can be tackled through tax policies.

Conclusion: You should reach your own conclusion about the issue based on the arguments and evidence presented. You need to justify your conclusion. You must not ignore what the writers say and simply present your own views.

`A possible conclusion might include:

- Jones is more concerned with the general economic situation while Nelson is also concerned with the problems of the lower paid.
- Jones is concerned with ways to raise large amounts of money, from higher taxes on the wealthy, – presumably to pay for additional services – but Nelson feels that the best way to stimulate the economy is by helping the lower paid with tax cuts and not punishing the wealthy.
- Both writers agree that Corporation Tax should be changed. Nelson wants it to be as low as possible, whereas Jones is happy to raise it but keep it lower than competitors.
- I think Nelson's argument is the more convincing because he is concerned about how the economic situation has affected ordinary people. Jones seems just anti-rich. Nelson seems to have a more balanced approach.

79 Practice linked theme question

Individual responses that might include some of the following points, for example.

Arguments to support the view may include:

- Democracy is based on the sovereignty of the people and government is elected by popular vote. People vote for representatives in elections, with different types of voting used for different elections. Direct democracy is when rule changes are made through referendums – a direct vote by the people. All four countries in the UK have representative democracy at national and local level.
- Regional assemblies in Wales and Scotland are elected using a form of proportional representation. This means that different views are represented in a way that reflects the proportion of people who support them. This contrasts with the first-past-the-post system used for the UK Parliament which means that sometimes the views of almost two-thirds of electors are not represented by their elected MP. Proportional representation is a more democratic system. It means that most electors feel there is somebody looking after their interests.
- The regional assemblies have constituencies which are numerically smaller than those for UK elections. This means that MPs can represent a smaller section of the population which allows people to have more chance of having their voices heard.
- The Scots and Welsh have strong national identities independent of the UK. In the UK government their national and cultural identities and interests can often be swamped by the majority control of English MPs. This is not very democratic. The Scots and Welsh with their own national assemblies means the interests of their own countries are given attention without the influence or distraction of English MPs.
- England has various regional identities which can be stronger than their national identity, but the UK Parliament is more

concerned with UK affairs and does not always consider English regional interests. English regional interests can be severely neglected. This is particularly true of the North and the West Country, where many people feel their views are not represented at all. Many would like to see regional assemblies for English regions with comparable powers to those of Scotland and Wales.

Arguments to counter the view may include:
- The first-past-the-post system is tried and tested. It discourages smaller political parties so that it is more likely that a government will have the support of the majority of the population, even if at the constituency level some people do not think their views are represented. Some may feel cheated and disenfranchised, but it usually gives a more stable government which doesn't depend on compromise to get the support of other parties.
- Scottish and Welsh MPs sit in the UK Parliament and can speak and vote on English affairs, but there are no English MPs in the Welsh or Scottish Assemblies. This means that England is more democratic than the other countries because it allows all parts of the UK to be represented in Parliament. Scottish and Welsh Assemblies can take decisions without taking account of the interests of people in the rest of the UK.
- The Scottish and Welsh Assemblies appear to be more democratic, but they can only do what the UK Parliament allows. Their powers and finance are delegated from Westminster and can always be recalled. This is not very democratic.
- England is more democratic because they only have one assembly to discuss all their affairs. In Scotland and Wales some things are discussed in the assembly but really important issues such as foreign affairs are discussed in London.

Conclusion
- England does not have the same level of democracy as the other two countries, but it has more control of Scotland and Wales than Scotland and Wales have over England.
- In Scotland and Wales there appears to be more democracy than in England because there is a closer relationship between voters and their assembly representative than there is in England, and they have closer control and power over local decisions.
- However, the sheer size of England means that the English MPs in Parliament are able to determine what happens in the other two countries.

Theme D: Power and influence

80 Citizen participation
Individual responses. For example:
1. Direct action through carrying out protest marches in the town.
2. Indirect action through writing letters and starting a petition to put pressure on councillors and their local MP.

81 Voter participation
Individual responses. For example:
1. They could increase efforts to provide information about candidates and how to vote. This could include personal meetings between voters and candidates.
2. They could make voting more accessible. For example, polling stations could be situated in supermarkets or at workplaces.

82 Participation outside the UK
Individual responses. For example: For a country to be truly democratic, voters must have a genuine choice of who to vote for, without fear. In one-party states such as North Korea there is not range of parties available and criticism of the government is likely to mean being sent to a prison camp.

83 Groups in democratic society
Individual responses. For example:
1. Pressure groups can represent causes that citizens care about and put pressure on the government to take their views into account when creating policy.
2. Trade unions can represent the interests of workers and can campaign against the government for improved pay and conditions.

84 Citizens working together
Individual responses. For example: Citizens can work in a group to resolve a local community issue. For example, if a local hospital is under threat of closure, a local group could organise mass demonstrations, lobby politicians and raise funds to challenge the decision and keep it open.

85 Protecting workplace rights
Individual responses. For example:
1. Trade unions are relevant today because they continue to protect and support the rights of people in the workplace. For example, they can use their collective action to negotiate with employers to improve pay and conditions.
2. Trade unions continue to use their knowledge of rights in the workplace to represent their members. For example, if an individual is in dispute with their employer, their trade union can represent them to protect their rights at a tribunal.

86 Democracy and the media
Individual responses. For example: It is important for democracy that accurate reporting keeps citizens well informed. When the media informs, it is giving the public the facts and reporting what is happening without expressing an opinion. When the media influences the public, it is trying to persuade them to see things in a particular way. It involves giving an opinion or presenting information in a biased way.

87 Media rights and regulation
Individual responses. For example:
1. Freedom of speech is an important right protected by the Human Rights Act 1998. This freedom allows the media to criticize government without fear of being prosecuted.
2. Self-regulation is sufficient and legislation is not needed to control their activity. Standards and Editors' Codes of Practice are in place through Impress and IPSO and these are adequate for regulation and control.

88 Media and influence
Individual responses. For example: Public opinion is the range of views held by the population in a country about what should be done. It is important because politicians in a democratic society need to represent their constituents and make their policies attractive to voters.

89 The UK and Europe
Individual responses. For example:
1. It promotes human rights, democracy and the rule of law.
2. It runs the European Court of Human Rights, which enforces the European Convention of Human Rights.

90 EU membership benefits and obligations
Individual responses. For example:
1. Free trade in the world's largest market.
2. Cooperation on policing and anti-terrorism laws.

91 Impact of EU decisions
Individual responses. For example: The EU has over 100 laws that help protect the environment. For example, EU rules have prevented UK water companies from pumping raw sewage into the sea. This means that now over 600 beaches meet the EU clean beach standard, providing a positive environment for people, wildlife and the ocean.

92 The UK's role in the world

Individual responses. For example:
1. As a leading member of the Commonwealth, the UK can influence Commonwealth aims including economic, social and sustainable development.
2. As a member of the World Trade Organization, the UK has a say on the rules that govern international trade.

93 Benefits and commitments

Individual responses. For example:
1. As a member, the UK enjoys improved trading conditions with other member countries. These include lower trade barriers, which helps consumers in the UK to buy cheaper goods.
2. Having a set of agreed rules should minimise the possibility of trade disputes. However, should conflicts arise, the WTO acts to help solve them.

94 Global responsibilities

Individual responses. For example:
1. Their right to life may be under threat from the fighting.
2. Children's rights may be violated if they are forced to fight against their will.

95 International law

Individual responses. For example: The International Criminal Court is separate from the UN and deals with the most serious crimes, such as genocide and crimes against humanity. The International Court of Justice is a United Nations body which is mainly concerned with disputes about territory or resources.

96 Non-governmental organisations

Individual responses. For example: NGOs are non-governmental organisations such as charities that are not run by governments, but may receive government money for their projects. For example, Water Aid is an NGO that uses its expertise in the water industry to help develop facilities in areas that lack them. They provide this humanitarian aid without expectation of any reward for themselves.

97 UK's role in international conflict

Individual responses. For example:
1. They can put economic pressure on a country that is breaking international law and force them to change policy by depriving them of essential goods.
2. They can refuse to sell military equipment to a country which is waging war and so can weaken their ability to continue fighting.

Paper 2 Section B: Power and influence (others' actions)

98–99 Source A questions

Individual responses. For example:
1. Andrew Mitchell said he accepted the need for new housing but he intended to carry on fighting the proposal to build on Sutton Coldfield's green belt land, implying they should be built somewhere else.
2. They were annoyed that a development had been forced on them by the council who ignored their objections. They don't seem bothered about where the houses should be built so long as it wasn't in Sutton Coldfield.

100 Short answer questions

Individual responses. For example:
1. They needed an extra 80,000 houses by 2030.
2. There was insufficient brownfield land in the city to build the houses needed.

101 Long answer question

Individual responses. For example:
1. As the local MP, he was a person of standing and influence in the community. His support might encourage more of his constituents and supporters to get involved.

2. As an MP he was part of Parliament and belonged to the governing party. He was in a position where he could try to influence the government to back the protesters. We had the support of our councillor who raised our issue at a council meeting.

103 Practice short answer questions

Explain question: Individual responses. For example:
1. They have removed fallen and decayed trees. This means that people using the wood will not trip over or be hit by falling branches.
2. They have repaired gates. This means that animals can't get into the woodland and it stops little children running into the roads.

Suggest question: Individual responses. For example:
1. Because the Friends have organised a number of activities to attract people.
2. Because it is now a lot safer and more attractive without the debris.

Analyse question: Individual responses. For example:
JLR is a major local employer that encourages its employees to get involved in charity work and volunteering.

104 Practice long answer question

Individual responses. For example:
- The group is made up of individuals who are volunteers. They have only a limited amount of time and manpower to reverse years of neglect. Volunteers have enthusiasm but not necessarily the knowledge and expertise needed to tackle some of the jobs.
- They need extra support and work, not paid for by the Friends. This was provided by JLR and council employees. The use of council employees implies they probably came from the parks department. Some of the tasks they needed to do such as felling and cutting up large trees require specialist equipment. The Friends would be unlikely to have access to this and so may have to depend on the council.
- Renovation of woodland is expensive as well as time consuming. Some volunteers have enthusiasm but lack forestry or construction ability/skills, so can use their skills as fundraisers.
- Fundraising also includes activities, so organisers and ideas are needed to attract the local population and raise extra funds. The project needs public and community support, not simply for activity days but to make use of the wood once renovated.
- The work develops a sense of local pride and ownership, making it more worthwhile. Note the support of the local MP. There are ongoing demands as the wood needs to be properly maintained and protected to avoid falling into disuse and decay again.

Paper 2 Section C: Power and influence

105 Multiple choice questions

The correct answer is **A**, a single-issue group. This is correct because a single-issue group is one which has a single aim, in this case stopping badger culling. **B** is not correct because it refers to groups having several aims and so does not fit with 'dedicated' in the question. **C** is not correct because promotional groups (sometimes called 'cause' groups) exist to promote a particular issue, such as Shelter and homelessness. **D** is not correct because the group would focus on human rights, not badger rights.

106 Short and long answers

1. To protect the employment rights of workers.
2. To negotiate collectively for workers' wages.
3. To support members who face disciplinary procedures at work.

107 Reasoned argument question

Individual responses. For example:
1. Raises awareness of issues among members of the public.
2. Puts pressure on those in power to make better or different decisions.
3. Is a method of engaging in democracy outside of elections.

09 Linked theme questions

Individual responses. For example:

- NATO still provides mutual support which could protect the UK against attack.
- Russia's aggressive foreign policy threatens world peace more than at any time in the last 30 years and western nations must unite if it is to be resisted.
- The UK isn't financially strong enough to maintain a military force which could resist a potential aggressor.

10 Practice short and long answers

Multiple choice question: The correct answer is C. The EU does not have its own armed force but encourages cooperation. The other answers give accurate descriptions of what membership of the EU gives.

Explain question (free press): Individual responses. For example: The law does not allow the press to print defamatory comments about individuals. Defamation is making false statements about a person which can harm their reputation.

Give question: Individual responses. For example:

- Giving an interview to a television reporter to present their ideas in a favourable way to a large audience.
- Paying for an advert in the newspapers which tells people about what they have done.

Explain question (leave EU): Individual responses. For example:

- The media was full of negative stories about the EU and its relationship with the UK. This made people think that the EU was the cause of many of the UK's problems.
- The UK contributes money to the EU as part of its membership. The Leave campaign promised that such money would be invested in the NHS if people voted to leave. People thought leaving would therefore help the NHS.

Explain question (UN/WTO): Individual responses that may include the below points, for example:

United Nations (UN)
- maintains international peace and security
- protects human rights
- delivers humanitarian aid
- promotes sustainable development
- upholds international law.

World Trade Organization (WTO)
- Aims to encourage world trade and prosperity.
- Encourages member countries to agree to rules of trade, settle trading disputes fairly, promote free trade between countries.
- Helps producers and consumers, importers and exporters, to trade efficiently.
- Cooperates with international organisations so that economies can grow.

11 Practice reasoned argument

Individual responses that may include some of the following points, for example:

- A democratic society is not a lawless society.
- The overriding principle is that no person or institution is above the law.
- The freedom of the press means freedom from government control or influence. It does not imply total freedom from any limitations.

Supporting the argument
- One role of the media is to expose corruption and illegal practices and hold government to account. Limitations may make this difficult or impossible. Limits placed by government would be contrary to the basis of a 'free press'.
- Restrictions are often imposed by those who fear exposure.
- Dictatorships control the media.
- Media is the main source of information for citizens and in the interests of democracy should not be limited.

- Social media is almost impossible to control so it is unfair for other media to be restricted.
- The aim of media is to give the audience what they want, which is not possible with more restrictions.
- Freedom of opinion and expression without interference or control is a basic human right.
- It is right that the media should be free to investigate anything in the public interest.
- Restricting information will limit the public's right to know and their ability to make proper choices.

Opposing the argument
- Freedom should not be total but should respect the rights and interests of others.
- Media should be subject to the same laws of libel, slander and decency as citizens.
- Media should be stopped from being untrue, harmful or from damaging individuals.
- Publication can cause great and unnecessary upset, for example the investigation by the BBC of Cliff Richard.
- The Press Council's self-regulation is useless and should be tightened up and given teeth. This was one result of the Leveson Inquiry.
- Censorship is sometimes needed, for example during war time, or in connection with security issues.
- The media is too powerful and has too much influence. It should be restricted.
- There is a lack of public trust in the accuracy and lack of bias in the media; 'fake news'.
- There is debate about how much information should be made available through the media.
- The media is driven too much by the profit motive and less by the desire to inform accurately.

112 Practice linked theme question

Individual responses. For example:
- Trade unions emerged during the 19th century, with the aim to protect workers' rights.
- At the time, conditions were generally dreadful and there were few employment laws.
- Government attitude was *laissez faire* – leaving things to take their own course without interference.

For
- Unions have achieved major improvements for workers in many industries.
- When at their strongest they were able to pressure employers and government (for example, the industrial actions of the 1970s and 1980s) and raised wages.
- The unions' role has been to ensure employers carry out their legal responsibilities concerning working conditions, pay, health and safety, and unfair dismissal.
- Unions provide protection to workers when they deal with redundancy, unfair dismissal, injury at work, and so on.
- Unions exist to protect workers. This is their main function and they are able to concentrate on it.
- Their power is based on an ultimate threat of strike action, which hits profitability.
- Unions also have a political arm. They helped found the Labour Party in 1900 and continue to have an influence on the Labour Party, although this has declined since the 1980s.
- Unions are not answerable to the electorate for their actions, only to their members. Political parties are committed to winning support of the electorate and unlikely to do things that will offend them, unless they have to.

Against
- Unions cannot pass laws but governments can. The only way to have legally enforceable standards is through legislation.
- Since the 1950s, many employment-related laws have improved conditions, for example minimum wages, equality acts, and health and safety at work.

- Unions may impose conditions on particular employers, but legislation can impose it on all.
- Governments will do what they can to win votes so they will pass employment laws.
- EU employment regulations are embedded in UK law.
- The power of trade unions has declined because of restrictive laws passed since the Thatcher government, and because of declining membership. It is now mainly public service workers who belong to unions. Many workplaces are small, making it difficult to organise workers into unions.
- Unions have become too embroiled in politics at the expense of protecting members' interests.
- Some workers feel they can get better protection through private insurance than through union membership.
- Government inspectors supervise workplaces and if necessary, act to see the law is observed, which was traditionally the role of unions.

Conclusion:
- Freedom to join a union is a basic human right. Unions have played an important role in introducing new legislation. Governments have often been slow to protect workers from their employers.
- While government does have the power to pass laws and develop protection for workers, it appears unions are likely to do more to push for pay increases and the development of better conditions and rights for workers. This is what unions were created for.

Theme E: Taking citizenship action

113 Your citizenship action

Individual responses, depending on your own citizenship issue, action and approaches. For example: It was democratic because we asked everyone to write down an issue that was important to them. We discussed each issue and voted to decide the issue we would address as a team.

114 Identifying an issue

Individual responses. For example:
1. It was difficult to get anybody to make suggestions. To help generate ideas we wrote out the names of the Themes and each member of the group chose one Theme and suggested an action to take and the reasons why.
2. Not everyone agreed, as one member wanted action based on **Democracy in the UK** (Theme B) but the rest of the group wanted action based on **Living together in the UK** (Theme A). Another group's action was based on **Democracy in the UK**, so we swapped our reluctant member for one from the other team.

115 Secondary research

Individual responses that may reflect the following points. For example: One secondary source we used was a newspaper article. We made sure it was recent so it had the most up-to-date information. We ensured it was reliable by checking that it gave a number of viewpoints and was not biased in favour of one particular opinion.

116 Primary research questions

Individual responses should choose key questions that are relevant to the chosen citizenship action and show why the development of the action depended on responses to them. Here is an example that relates to the citizenship action about congestion (page 115) and key primary research questions (page 117): Our most important questions were: 'How far do you agree with the problems identified?' and 'Do you think that congestion is so bad that something should be done about it?' These were most important because the whole action was meant to identify the causes, and stop them being a problem. The action taken needed the support of the residents and road users. We needed to know what people thought about it before carrying out our action.

117 Primary research

Individual responses relevant to the chosen citizenship action and primary research.
Here is an example that relates to the citizenship action that organises a mock election to raise awareness among students of the nature of parliamentary elections (page 115):
We used agree/disagree statements in a questionnaire, and also conducted a poll to find out voter intentions. The questionnaire showed what people thought important. The candidates used the results in their election speeches.

118 Analysing primary research

Individual responses. For example: Primary research establishes new information using qualitative and quantitative methods. You find it out yourself. Secondary research is when you use evidence discovered and presented by somebody else. It already exists.

119 Representing viewpoints

Individual responses related to your own citizenship action. Here is an example:
1. We were careful to discuss everybody's suggestions and listen to what they had to say. We agreed not to interrupt or suggest that any ideas were silly.
2. When everybody had their chance to speak and ask questions we decided to take a vote on which plan to use. We agreed democratically that we would all accept the plan which had most votes.

120 Reviewing viewpoints

Individual responses based on your citizenship proposals and action plan. For example:
We had two different proposals. One person wanted to raise awareness but the other thought we should do a social action. The two advocates presented their ideas, telling us what we would have to do and what it would achieve. We then discussed the two plans and concentrated on which was the most achievable in the time we had. We then took a vote and agreed to do the awareness-raising activity because it had most support.

121 Planning the action

Individual responses, depending on citizenship action and target audience. Here is an example in relation to the citizenship action to raise student awareness of the disturbance caused to local residents at home time (page 115):
We wanted to raise student awareness of how their behaviour could cause distress to local residents, and encourage students to behave in a more considerate way.

122 Planning tasks and roles

Individual responses, depending on citizenship action and roles required. For example:
1. At first, we asked people to sign up for the tasks they wanted to do. This didn't work because too many people wanted to do some things but nobody wanted to do other things.
2. We then agreed that everyone would take one of the unpopular jobs as well as a job they wanted. We asked our team leader to give each person a job.

123 Applying skills in action

Individual responses, depending on citizenship action. Here is an example in the context of a presentation:
1. We demonstrated collaboration in our activity by sharing out the presentation between us. One of us introduced our citizenship action. Two other team members explained the benefits of what we proposed, and our fourth member explained the resources we wanted our audience to provide.
2. At the end we invited the audience to ask questions and then took it in turns to answer them. Each team member answered questions relating to the part of the action they had been responsible for.

124 Carrying out the action

Individual responses, depending on citizenship action. Here is an example in the context of a mock election (page 115): We held a mock election to inform our class about the voting system. Part of our presentation explained how voting was organised. One of our team talked to the class. Some people did not listen and didn't know what to do when it came to voting. If we did it again I would do it much more as a question and answer session to get people involved and thinking. Afterwards I would give them some sort of test, maybe a simple crossword, word search or 'filling in the gaps' to make sure that they understood what we told them.

125 Evaluating the action

Individual responses, depending on citizenship action. Here is an example, based on the congestion action on page 115, of some points you could assess your answer against.

We all agreed that we wanted to do something about the problem of congestion near our school. Malik lives in the road and explained to us some of the problems. Until he told us about it, we hadn't really thought about it, so communication was important. We discussed what to do and decided to present a petition to the council asking them to stop people parking near the school, because they were the only ones who could do anything practical.

As the work progressed, we held regular meetings to discuss what we had done and what still needed to be done. Alex thought this was a waste of time because he thought we ought to be out in the street interviewing drivers and house owners. We explained that the best way to get things done was to keep each other informed about progress.

One of the problems we found later on was that we couldn't always remember what we had agreed and who had done what. It came to a head when Chris tried to interview the councillor and found that he got cross because he had already talked to Jakub about the petition. He said we needed to get our act together.

Doing it again we would want to keep a record of everything we agreed. We could have made a chart to show what was to be done, who was to do it and the deadline. This would avoid confusion and repetition. Some of the team were so confused they lost interest.

Kavita started to do things without telling us what she had done. We should have agreed to work in pairs and give regular feedback to the rest of the group. To be effective as a group we needed to collaborate better. We found it worked best when we talked to each other.

Some of the team thought we spent too much time in discussion but others were unclear about what had to be done. We would have worked better if we had a strict timetable for discussions and made sure that we kept focused and didn't just talk for the sake of talking. We should have had a chairperson to control discussion and reach a positive outcome.

When it came to planning the final presentation, we realised that we knew what we wanted to do but weren't too sure how to do it. The way we solved this was by sitting down in a group and discussing it.

Good communication is very important, but it was just as vital that the methods we chose were effective. In the end we presented a petition to the council signed by most of the residents in the road. We wouldn't have been able to do this if we hadn't kept everybody informed of what we were doing. I think the two things are just as important, but we should have been more careful to keep a tighter focus so that communication was effective but didn't take up too much time, and the things we did were better controlled.

Paper 2 Section A: Own citizenship action

126 Section A questions

Individual responses, based on the choice of citizenship action. Here is an example, based on the example action for Theme A3 shown on page 127: Petitioning a shop owner to lift his ban on groups of teenagers being in the shop:

We decided we would make a petition and present it to the shopkeeper and ask him to lift his ban on groups of teenagers in his shop. We decided to do this because it is the only sweet shop near our school. We thought it unfair that we were all treated like criminals because of the misbehaviour of a few people. We wanted to show him that we were responsible and reasonable people, most of whom gave him regular custom and did not cause any problems.

127 Short answer questions

Individual responses that may be quantitative or qualitative, depending on your choice and citizenship action. For example, based on titles on page 127:

Quantitative answer: Quantitative evidence is based on numbers. For example, it allows you to compare the number of people who support an idea with those who don't and who aren't interested. It was useful because it showed that 28 of our class thought that students should have a say in rewriting the school rules. This was useful evidence when we spoke about our action to the Principal.

Qualitative answer: For qualitative evidence we completed a questionnaire with students in our class to find out what they knew about voting rights and political involvement from those aged 16. This showed us what the students thought and what we would need to explain to them to increase their knowledge of the arguments for votes at 16.

128 Long answer question

Individual responses. The points below are based on the example of citizenship action for Theme D, on page 127, against which you can review the kind of points you have made in relation to your own citizenship action.

- Most of us wanted our citizenship action to be about selling the school fields but James said we should try to get school uniform changed. We tried to explain that selling the fields would affect us all but he didn't like PE and said it was not important. When we tried to take a vote, he kept on arguing and wasting time, which was unfair.
- James is entitled to his view but as a team member he should accept the majority view. Further discussion should be about improving detail. It is not democratic to try to change decisions once they have been agreed.
- It is important to have different perspectives when deciding on an action. It is also good to have different ideas about how things should be done, but it is not good to undermine what most team members want.
- James probably was sincere in his views but he wasn't prepared to listen to what we all wanted. The time to argue is before decisions are made and not afterwards.
- We wanted James to help us plan what to do but his constant arguing led to conflict and bad feeling. Some of the team lost interest and didn't pull their weight later on. These arguments meant we didn't finish our action on time and failed to achieve our objectives.
- Conclusion: it is important to have different ideas and viewpoints when discussing what to do, but there comes a time when it is more important to accept a majority decision and get on with the work, even if you are not happy about some of the decisions. Teamwork is about collaboration and working together, so James' attitude had a negative impact and did not help us.

129 Practice short answers

Your citizenship action: Make sure that your title is not more than 20 words and it clearly shows the action and the course Theme and topic that it links with.

Explain question (teamwork): Individual responses. For example:

Close friends usually share similar interests and think the same way. In teamwork it is important to have different points of view and a variety of ideas.

Explain question (primary research): Individual responses. For example:

For our citizenship action we wanted to interview people in the street. When we worked in pairs one of us could ask questions and the other could write down answers.

Explain question (criteria for successful citizenship action): Individual responses. For example:

1. Our action was to raise a petition about the local shop's ban on groups of students. Our first criteria was the number of people we could persuade to sign the petition. We realised that the more signatures we had the more persuasive the petition would be.
2. Our second criteria was to have as much publicity as possible in order to increase the pressure on the shopkeeper. We decided to invite the local radio station and the local newspaper to send reporters when we presented the petition. The measure of success was if either of them attended and then published a report on our action.

Explain question (person of authority): Individual responses. For example:

One way in which this was helpful:
We arranged a meeting with the Head Teacher and the Chair of School Governors to talk about the plan to sell off the school playing fields. It was useful because they explained to us why the school had to sell the fields to raise money. They talked about the lack of funds and some alternatives they had considered.

One way in which this was difficult:
Negotiation with them was difficult because they were very busy and had to cancel the meeting several times. When it took place, we felt there wasn't enough time to explain our action or try to persuade them to support our ideas, though we kept our points short and asked if they would give us a link to further information on the internet.

130 Practice long answers

Individual responses. The example gives some key points in relation to the example citizenship action for Theme A on page 127. You can use the qualities in these points to evaluate your own response.

- For our citizenship action (organising a petition to a shopkeeper) we listed all the jobs that needed to be done on a sign-up sheet. Everyone had the chance to sign up for the tasks they wanted to do. Some jobs had three or four names and other jobs didn't have any names against them. To make progress, each person was allowed to choose three different jobs, in a preferred order, but this still left some jobs not allocated. This caused arguments as people did not want to do some tasks when other people got to choose what they wanted to do. We tried to see if we could just ignore the unpopular jobs but they were still important and still needed completing, so we decided to rethink.
- Later, Sue said she had worked out who should do which job and distributed lists. All the jobs were allocated and nobody was left out. Nobody had asked her to do this and some people complained that it was unfair, but we decided to try it. Some agreed to swap some of the jobs privately so they could do what they were happiest with. Eventually the plan worked and we managed to complete our action. Allocation by one person meant that all jobs were allocated and everybody had something to do. It saved time and was more efficient, avoiding argument about who wanted what, and made sure that people given jobs had the appropriate skills.
- However, this gave a lot of power to one person, potentially too much, and took away the freedom and initiative for people to choose what they wanted among themselves. Letting people volunteer may mean not all jobs are covered and that people may be unhappy if they don't get what they want. It can waste time in discussion and organisation and it may be delayed by people who can't be bothered to sign up. However, it is more democratic and less likely to lead to argument, building on individual enthusiasm and interest. It is important that everybody feels they are participating. If one person decides, they may seem more important and everybody else less important. They may favour friends over other members in the group, and it may result in unbalanced allocation as some get more to do and some get less.
- To evaluate our action, we talked about how roles were allocated, and overall, we thought that having one person choosing roles meant that all the jobs got done. At the same time this meant some people were unhappy that they didn't get what they wanted which was not democratic. We felt that teamwork should be more of a collaboration rather than a dictatorship.
- In conclusion, when Sue took over and dictated what others should do, it led to disagreement and argument in the group. This affected everyone's performance. For this approach to succeed it has to be based on discussion and agreement. We would have been happier if Sue had offered to do the job and then asked for our agreement. She should also have asked people what they wanted to do and what they preferred not to. This would have saved a lot of bad feeling and kept a positive approach within the group.

Notes

Notes

Notes

Notes

Notes

Notes